History of the Vikings

An Enthralling Overview of the Viking Age

© Copyright 2023 - All rights reserved.

The content contained within this book may not be reproduced, duplicated, or transmitted without direct written permission from the author or the publisher.

Under no circumstances will any blame or legal responsibility be held against the publisher, or author, for any damages, reparation, or monetary loss due to the information contained within this book, either directly or indirectly.

Legal Notice:

This book is copyright protected. It is only for personal use. You cannot amend, distribute, sell, use, quote, or paraphrase any part, or the content within this book, without the consent of the author or publisher.

Disclaimer Notice:

Please note the information contained within this document is for educational and entertainment purposes only. All effort has been executed to present accurate, up-to-date, reliable, and complete information. No warranties of any kind are declared or implied. Readers acknowledge that the author is not engaging in the rendering of legal, financial, medical, or professional advice. The content within this book has been derived from various sources. Please consult a licensed professional before attempting any techniques outlined in this book.

By reading this document, the reader agrees that under no circumstances is the author responsible for any losses, direct or indirect, that are incurred as a result of the use of the information contained within this document, including, but not limited to, errors, omissions, or inaccuracies.

Free limited time bonus

Stop for a moment. We have a free bonus set up for you. The problem is this: we forget 90% of everything that we read after 7 days. Crazy fact, right? Here's the solution: we've created a printable, 1-page pdf summary for this book that you're reading now. All you have to do to get your free pdf summary is to go to the following website:

https://livetolearn.lpages.co/enthrallinghistory/

Once you do, it will be intuitive. Enjoy, and thank you!

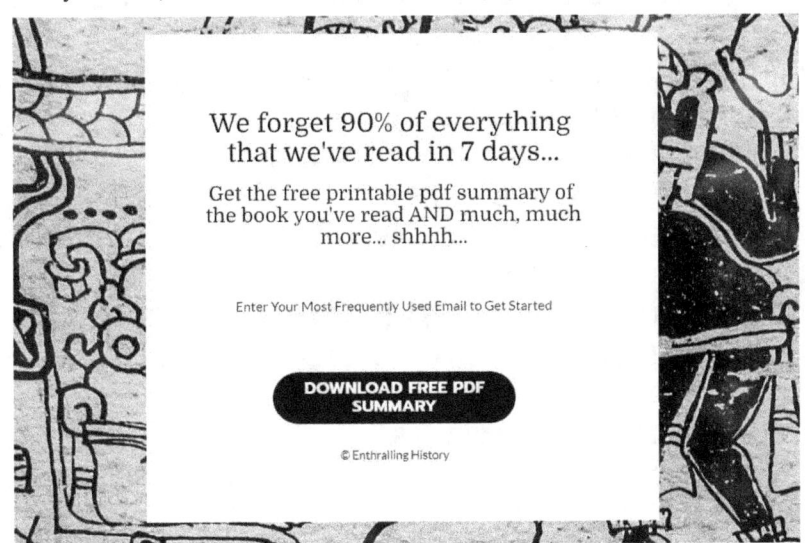

Table of Contents

INTRODUCTION 1
PART ONE: THE VIKING AGE: AN OVERVIEW (793–1066 CE) 3
CHAPTER 1: WHO WERE THE VIKINGS? 4
CHAPTER 2: WHAT WAS THE VIKING AGE? 12
CHAPTER 3: VIKING CONQUESTS 20
CHAPTER 4: THE FALL OF THE VIKINGS 30
PART TWO: REGULAR VIKING LIFE 38
CHAPTER 5: SOCIETAL STRUCTURE 39
CHAPTER 6: VILLAGE LIFE 46
CHAPTER 7: LITERATURE AND THE RUNIC ALPHABET 54
CHAPTER 8: ART, DESIGN, AND ARCHITECTURE 62
PART THREE: WARFARE AND WEAPONRY 70
CHAPTER 9: KEY VIKING BATTLES 71
CHAPTER 10: ARMOR AND WEAPONS 77
CHAPTER 11: VIKING SHIPS 84
CHAPTER 12: MORE THAN WARRIORS - VIKING TRADERS 93
PART FOUR: MYTH AND MYTHOLOGY 100
CHAPTER 13: CUSTOMS, RITUALS, AND RELIGION 101
CHAPTER 14: WARS OF THE GODS 109
CHAPTER 15: THE NINE REALMS IN NORSE MYTHOLOGY 116
CHAPTER 16: SYMBOLS AND POSSESSIONS OF THE NORSE GODS AND GODDESSES 124

CONCLUSION 132
HERE'S ANOTHER BOOK BY ENTHRALLING HISTORY THAT
YOU MIGHT LIKE 133
FREE LIMITED TIME BONUS 134
BIBLIOGRAPHY 135

Introduction

Vikings, warriors, Norse peoples, Scandinavians, and more are all terms used interchangeably when referring to the people who lived in present-day Scandinavia during the height of the Viking Age. Not all of those terms apply to the Vikings. Only those who participated in the raids were Vikings because they went "a viking." However, the people of Scandinavia and elsewhere were part of the collective Viking experience.

Because of the Vikings' amazing accomplishments and daring feats, they are one of the most well-known groups of people from our collective past. Their escapades are inspirational. An independent spirit gave these Scandinavian peoples the strength and vision to explore the world beyond their immediate shores.

Beyond raiding and pillaging, their sailing adventures fostered incredible craftsmen. Shipbuilding and the navigational tools they developed show their understanding of the natural world around them. Their weaponry demonstrated the same intellectual curiosity and ability to create devices that were well made and met their needs.

Vikings are often depicted as lawless savage combatants. Yes, they certainly left many quivering in their wake. But once they settled in an area they seized, the Scandinavians brought respect, leading to the beginnings of a democracy. They had laws they followed, retribution for lawbreakers, and assemblies in which villagers had input.

The Scandinavians had expectations of how each person should be treated. A strong work ethic and living an honorable life were among the virtues they extolled. No, they were not perfect, but they were also not bloodthirsty monsters.

Gods and goddesses helped guide their way. Deeply rooted belief systems gave their lives purpose, and their belief in an afterlife for honorable warriors in Valhalla guided combatants into battle. The nine realms of the Viking world framed their connections to their deities, ancestors, and origins.

Understanding people who came before us is important for us to know more about ourselves. We may not agree with all of their beliefs, but framing their principles in their time period is critical to gaining insight into other cultures.

PART ONE: The Viking Age: An Overview (793–1066 CE)

Chapter 1: Who Were the Vikings?

On June 8th, 793 CE, the first recorded attack by the Vikings on European soil occurred. The Vikings seemingly materialized out of thin air and brutally assaulted the monastery on the island of Lindisfarne, which is located off the northeast coast of England. The Viking Age and the terror that accompanied it began on that day.

Magic and sorcery did not cause the Vikings to suddenly appear on that island. Archaeologists have pieced together what they believe to be the origins of the Vikings, the culture that became infamous for their fearsome raids. However, their ancestors had thrived for thousands of years before the Viking Age.

Land formations that resulted from the Ice Age made parts of the area known today as Scandinavia habitable to early humans. This transformation occurred over twelve thousand years ago and is classified as the Stone Age. For thousands of years, sections of Scandinavia were populated by hunters and gatherers. Ancient peoples migrated from modern Europe, Syria, and Russia.

During the Bronze Age, the ancestors of the Vikings developed metalworking skills. They became adept at fashioning tools that were much stronger and accomplished more tasks. With the development of new tools, sturdier buildings were constructed. Because of this, a shift from nomadic hunters and gatherers occurred, with more people farming. Additionally, a more structured and hierarchical society began to emerge around 1700 BCE.

Rock carving from Sweden.
https://en.m.wikipedia.org/wiki/File:Scandinavian_Civilization_-_rock_carvings.jpg

Much of the interpretation of how the people of the Scandinavian Bronze Age lived has been provided through the analysis of petroglyphs. Petroglyphs are rock carvings. Originally, many believed the petroglyphs were etched by the ancestors of the Vikings; however, more current research shows the carvings to be from the Bronze Age. This new interpretation of the evidence suggests that cultures traded extensively with each other during the Bronze Age.

To facilitate trade and transactions, ships carried the buyers or sellers and their goods to other countries. The Norse built ships of varying sizes. From the cave drawings, it is believed that the largest ships made by Viking ancestors had the capacity for a crew of over fifty.

Due to the growing trade, other countries became acquainted with their northern neighbors. Pliny the Elder, an ancient Roman historian, is believed to have referred to the lands of Norway and Sweden as Scatinavia when he described the territories he encountered. Later, the Greek explorer Pytheas called the lands Scandiae.

The people of the lands known as Scandinavia would continue to develop their trade with other countries during the Iron Age, which occurred between 500 BCE and 800 CE. Scandinavians prospered due to increased trade with other cultures and lands during this time, including the Roman Empire. Some settlements in Scandinavia transformed into trade centers to accommodate the needs of buyers and sellers.

Iron was even stronger than the metals used by people during the Bronze Age, and the new metal transformed many ancient societies. More communities were settled during the Iron Age partly because iron tools made farming and building easier.

The application of iron went beyond its use as implements to feed, cloth, and shelter inhabitants. Iron was also utilized for weapons. With the ability to readily produce iron devices, powerful weapons were available for the multitudes. An increase in warfare was one result of the proliferation of iron-based weaponry.

Also, during the Iron Age, the demise of the Western Roman Empire occurred. In 476 CE, Rome fell. Without the strong government in Rome controlling much of Europe, regional conflicts emerged. Many smaller kingdoms arose, which all vied for power and land. Roadways between villages were no longer maintained, making traveling and trade a challenge. Seaways were no longer under the control of the Roman Empire, increasing the power of pirates and other cultures.

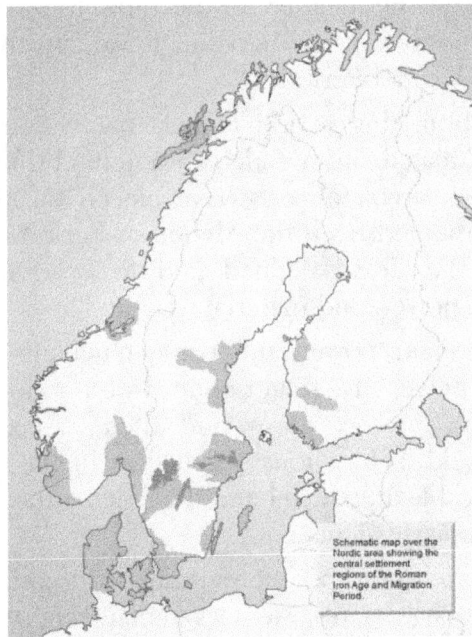

Map of Scandinavian settlements during the Migration Period.
https://commons.wikimedia.org/wiki/File:Nordic_Settlements.gif

The Migration Period helped bring about the decline and ultimate fall of the Western Roman Empire. During the years between 300 to 700 CE, thousands of tribes migrated throughout Europe. Numerous Germanic tribes, which are credited with the collapse of Rome, reshaped the political and cultural landscape of Europe. The transformation from centralized to decentralized governance caused the formation of numerous small territories or kingdoms. Continual warfare between the leaders resulted.

Scandinavia's once bountiful trade with Europe plummeted precipitously. Evidence found by archaeologists suggests that its wealth and economic prosperity declined dramatically throughout the Migration Period. Excavations of gravesites revealed many buried treasures with the dead. Hiding family valuables in this manner supports theories of political unrest, which was similar to what was occurring in Europe. It is believed that families felt they were protecting their wealth during this unsettled time.

Scandinavian society was also experiencing societal instability, with its structure being challenged. A shift from small farms and villages to a more tiered society with fewer decision-makers emerged. Influential families battled for the chance to become the ruling elite. This transitional time between the Migration Period to the Viking Age is referred to as the Vendel Period.

Information about this period and its name come from ancient burial grounds located in Vendel, Sweden. From this site and Valsgärde, Sweden, archaeologists have pieced together elements of the society that emerged from the Migration Period and set the stage for the Viking Age. Ideals valued and fostered during this time included prestige, power, and material wealth.

To gain and retain power, the rising chieftains or jarls had to consolidate their power. To retain control of a region, rulers needed strong warriors to protect them and their assets. Meetings and gatherings were held in longhouses that the chieftains built. In these great halls, the local leaders exhibited their status through lavish feasts and wearing dazzling garments.

Local farmers and tradespeople were invited to religious rituals and celebrations. The jarl's status was elevated through these displays of grandeur. Leaders also used these occurrences to demonstrate the strength of their warriors. With the continually shifting allegiances, a region and its jarl needed powerful combatants to protect their people and their lands. Chieftains continually had to prove their ability to defeat others who attacked. Any signs of weakness were detrimental to a leader's survival.

Construction of hill and ring forts for protection began during the Vendel Period. Usually circular in construction, these fortified structures stored food and animals. Villagers stayed in the forts when their homes were under attack. And this happened more and more as neighboring leaders battled each other for dominance of the region.

Military objects discovered in graves throughout the area illustrate the artistry of the people and their growing reverence for the warriors. Helmets won by warriors demonstrated the status of their military prowess. These helmets were adorned with precious gems and inscribed with scenes from myths of the Scandinavian people. Vendel Period helmets encompass the evolving beliefs and goals of the time.

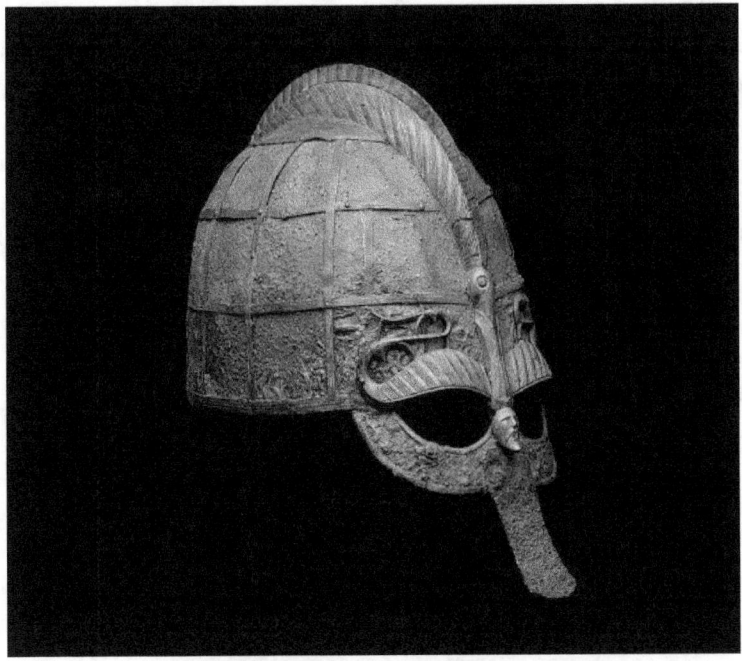

Helmet from the Vendel Period.
Ola Myrin/Statens historiska museum, CC BY 2.5
<*https://creativecommons.org/licenses/by/2.5*>, *via Wikimedia Commons*
https://commons.wikimedia.org/wiki/File:Vendel_I_helmet_456059.jpg

In addition to stunning helmets, Scandinavian craftspeople were adroit at working with many metals. Artisans created works in gold, bronze, and iron, and the tradespeople were instrumental in the resurgence of trade, which had floundered since the fall of Rome. The ability to trade goods and import treasures from other lands added to the status of the jarl or chieftain. Winning victories in battles, displaying wealth, hosting lavish feasts in the longhouse, and protecting the people in his region ensured that the chieftain retained his position of power. Longevity and support of the locals were required by the jarl if he wanted to become king.

The glorification of warriors in the Scandinavian culture leading up to the Viking Age can be found in the epic poem *Beowulf*. The only known written version of the poem is from 1000 CE. Though it was one of the first pieces of Anglo-Saxon writing, the setting of the tale is the lands of Scandinavia. Historical figures, such as Danish King Hrothgar, provide researchers with an estimate of when the bards told the poem.

No evidence exists that Beowulf was an actual person. Perhaps he was a compilation of various warriors who ate, drank, and celebrated victories in the great halls of the Scandinavian kings. The traveling storytellers would have shared the incredible feats accomplished by Beowulf as they journeyed from village to village. Good fought evil in the form of Beowulf conquering monsters. He eliminated Grendel, "a creature of darkness," as well as Grendel's mother. To save others, Beowulf slayed a dragon, which ended his life.

The first page of Beowulf, dated roughly 1000.
https://commons.wikimedia.org/wiki/File:Beowulf_Cotton_MS_Vitellius_A_XV_f._132r.jpg

The looting and plundering that characterized the Viking Age were depicted in the story of *Beowulf*. Beowulf's larger-than-life exploits would transfer into tales of real-life warriors taking on the world.

At the inception of the Viking Age, the Vikings did not refer to themselves as Vikings. They were also not unified under the auspices of one king or leader. Each region was separated into different tribes or clans. People were loyal to their local chieftain or jarl. Most villagers lived and worked on their farms or as tradespeople. Karls were the free landowners of Scandinavian society who participated in Viking raids. Servants and enslaved people were referred to as thralls.

The people's lives followed the seasons and the cycle of farming. Spring was planting season, and crops were harvested in the fall. Cold and dark winters were times of sheltering in longhouses. Stories of the summer exploits of trading and pillaging were shared over winter fires. These tales perpetuated the glory of raiding and ensured the sequence would repeat itself the next summer.

The definitive origin of the term "Viking" is unknown, but many scholars feel its root is the Norse word *vík*. Other words closely related to *vík* include *vika* and *víkja*; these words are all connected to the sea. *Víkingr* was used to denote a seafaring adventurer in Old Norse. This term has been found in stories, poetry, and runestones, which were written using the runic alphabet. These inscriptions detail the exploits of people during this time. When the term *Víkingr* is carved, it indicates a seafaring warrior, not an entire group of people.

Some of those impacted by the Viking invasions began to refer to the attacking forces as Vikings. Wiccinga or Wiccingi, which is the singular and plural form of Viking in Latin, has been discovered in the writing of monks living in England during the attacks. Initially, other countries called the warriors the Danes, though not all Vikings were from Denmark. The foreigners, Northmen, Majūs for mysterious and misunderstood, heathens, and other monikers have all been replaced by the term Viking.

The majority of Scandinavians were not Vikings and never participated in any raids. Only those who partook in the pillaging adventures at sea were Vikings. Other Scandinavians traveled as merchants, trading and bartering goods from their homeland with those in other lands. The tradespeople that the Scandinavians encountered called them Northmen or Norsemen to refer to their region of origin.

Saga Oseberg, a replica of a Viking ship.
https://www.pexels.com/photo/close-up-of-the-saga-oseberg-8876097/

For almost three hundred years, the Vikings ruled the seaways. When their impressive ships approached, shouts of the "Vikings are coming!" or the "Vikings have arrived!" sent waves of fear and terror throughout the land.

The Vikings landed in more than forty countries and territories. They founded market towns to trade their goods and initiated a global trading network. Their influence on laws and instilling justice have had a lasting impact. Their shipbuilding skills and spirit of adventure led them to discover lands that were unknown to them, such as Greenland and Iceland. Scandinavian technology enabled them to reach North America before Christopher Columbus.

Numerous theories have been explored to determine the events that precipitated the Vikings to begin their raids. Overpopulation, lack of quality farmland, a desire for silver, and a sense of adventure may have all contributed to the raids. Regardless of the reasons, the Vikings had an indelible impact on communities in Europe, especially in England. After the days of surprise attacks on villages ended, Vikings effected changes throughout all levels of society.

Chapter 2: What Was the Viking Age?

The years from 793 to 1066 CE are the dates typically associated with the Viking Age. The year 793 saw the first documented Viking raid. The Vikings attacked Lindisfarne, a monastery off the coast of England.

The Vikings were notorious for their sudden and frightening attacks on towns throughout Europe. They did more than raid and pillage. Vikings also settled in villages, vastly expanded their trading routes, and explored lands previously unknown to them.

Especially at the beginning of the Viking Age, the Vikings did not sail as a cohesive group representing all of the current Scandinavian countries. Scandinavians shared a common language, ancestry, and skill in navigation and shipbuilding. The geography of their region dictated the development of their ability to build ships and traverse waterways.

People living in Sweden, Norway, and Denmark had vastly different land formations to contend with. However, the territories all had watercourses, thickly forested regions, and impenetrable mountains.

Picture of a Norwegian fjord.
https://unsplash.com/photos/W1FIkdPAB7E

Waterways included fjords, which were formed from glaciers. Fjords are incredibly deep inlets and provide narrow openings to the sea. They are bordered by steep sides of rocks that form cliffs. These challenging topographical features necessitated water travel as the most effective method of transportation.

Other topographical features of the land created a natural separation between tribes. Norsemen in Norway contended with narrow strips of farmland between the edges of fjords and mountains. Similarly, Sweden was challenged by small sections of fertile land situated between waterways and mountains. Colder temperatures added to the difficulties of farm life. Denmark had the best land for growing crops and was in a good location for contact beyond Scandinavia.

These geographical conditions developed strong regional ties in Scandinavia as the people entered the Viking Age. Some of these circumstances may have fostered the need to explore other regions.

Numerous factors are believed to have led to the initial raids that are emblematic of the Viking Age. The Scandinavians' navigational and ship-making prowess contributed to the expansion of the Scandinavian world and the success of the raids.

The growing population in the years preceding the Viking Age, along with limited farmable land, may have been one of the contributing factors to the Viking raids. Young men were likely willing to sail on Viking ships with the hope of finding new lands to farm. Adding to the complexity of sufficient farmable land was the practice of primogeniture. In this system, the eldest son inherited the family's entire estate. Any other sons in the family were left landless. This may have inspired males without land to inherit to join the expeditions.

Landowners held the power in Scandinavian societies. However, for a family to differentiate itself from other landowners, it had to amass more wealth than farming alone would have provided. For those seeking the role of local chieftain or jarl, he had to seek materials obtained from other lands and countries, which would add to his status. Fine clothing, unusual treasures, lavish feasts, and an ornate longhouse advanced one's position and importance. Goods obtained from Viking raids provided a means for new landowners to secure more power.

Continual struggles for control and shifting alliances created political turmoil. Chieftains sought to add land to their regions of control. Kings pursued even more dominance and strove to consolidate multiple chieftains under their rule. Jarls who did not want to be controlled by a king relinquished their power. These jarls joined Viking treks and settled new lands in other countries. Some jarls were exiled when they lost a power struggle; others voluntarily left to begin anew.

Not only chieftains desired adventure. The Scandinavians' spirit of independence and bravery led them to be enticed by the sea. Visiting faraway lands gave those seeking escape from their structured and tiered society new ambitions. They would return to their homeland with extraordinary tales of new worlds and exotic goods, adding invaluable status to these legendary pioneers. An added benefit for the explorers was the belief in Valhalla, the Norse religion's equivalent of heaven. Dying in battle ensured the deceased would be escorted to Valhalla by Odin, the Norse god of war and the dead.

Though not clearly documented, it is thought that the initial Viking raids sailed from Norway and arrived in England and Ireland in 750. In the years that followed, ships launched from Denmark and often disembarked in southeastern England, the Netherlands, and France. Vikings who voyaged from Sweden typically sailed east toward the Baltics and Russia. It is believed that during the early years of the raids, the ships frequently followed the coastline. However, due to the talent of the Vikings, their shipbuilding expertise, and advancements in nautical technology, the open seas soon became navigable.

Exploratory raiding parties of Vikings are thought to have begun as early as 750. There is some evidence of Norse ships landing in Kent and Wessex in 753 and 788 or 789, respectively, which supports the theory of raids occurring before 793. Over the next few decades, northern England experienced bouts of looting and small-scale raids. The intensity of the raids grew, with the first documented large-scale invasion occurring in 793. For many, this date marks the official commencement of the Viking Age.

Information about the earliest raids and the attack on Lindisfarne Priory was documented in the *Anglo-Saxon Chronicle*. In approximately 890, King Alfred the Great commissioned the recording of events that had occurred in England. The *Anglo-Saxon Chronicle* recounts events beginning in 60 BCE.

The Viking Raiding Stone is known by many names, including the Lindisfarne Stone or Doomsday Stone. This gravestone is believed to depict the events that transpired on that June day in 793. The gravestone was discovered at the priory. Carvings in the stone depict a group of warriors with Viking-like weapons. The other side of the stone reveals celestial images and figures that appear to be praying. Conjectures imply that the side of the stone with warriors represents the Vikings who attacked; the other face of the grave marker depicts the monks in prayer.

Adding to the validity of details of the raid that launched the Viking Age are the writings of Alcuin of York. A well-known scholar, clergyman, and Palatine school educator at Charlemagne's court, Alcuin was contacted via letter by the bishop of Lindisfarne with details of the attack. In Alcin's reply to Bishop Higbald's correspondence, he expresses his grief and horror over the ghastly raid on the monastery.

Only Alcin's letter still exists. In it, he included details about the attack being made by pagans, which is a reference to the Vikings. He also expressed his surprise that a raid could happen at the priory due to its distance from the sea. Alcin noted that St. Cuthbert's Church, which was at Lindisfarne, was desecrated with the blood of the monks and looted of its chalices, crosses, and other goods that demonstrated devotion to God.

While the strike on the monastery shocked the monks and others, many researchers do not believe it was a random act executed by the Vikings. The priory was founded by St. Aidan in 634 CE and was well-known within the Christian community. Visitors frequently worshiped there.

In addition to being houses of worship, Christian monasteries provided areas for learning and literature. Collections of indelible books and manuscripts, often hand-copied by monks in beautiful calligraphy and ornate decorations, were located at these holy sites. Hand-woven and embroidered fabrics, golden chalices, and gem-ladened goblets, which were all used in religious ceremonies, were housed at thriving monasteries.

As a hub of worship, Lindisfarne flourished in 793. However, the Kingdom of Northumbria, where the Holy Island of Lindisfarne was located, was undergoing turmoil in its leadership. In the fifty-eight years leading up to the attack and for almost a decade after the Vikings' arrival, ten different kings led the territory. Continual battles between rivals caused the deposition of each king.

Ominous storms started the year for the residents of Northumbria, followed by a deadly famine. Both seemed to be a foreshadowing of the catastrophic events of June 793.

Norsemen often sailed their regular trade route, which was along the coast of England. This provided the Vikings with a familiarity of the area's terrain, the ongoing upheaval in Northumbria, and experience with the sea route to and from the Holy Island. It is thought the Vikings planned their attack on the monastery because of their depth of knowledge of the situation.

Most likely, three or four ships with a total of upward of one hundred Vikings participated in the raid on Lindisfarne. Vikings sailed in longships when going on raids. In addition to speed, these ships could land on beaches, allowing the Vikings to attack more easily. Prows, the forward section of the ship's bow that was above water, were often carved to look like dragons.

On the morning of June 8th, 793 CE, the monks may have been sleeping, in the church praying, illuminating manuscripts, or tilling the fields. Suddenly, the chapel bells rang out, warning all of the inhabitants of the island. Monks looked over the walls of the monastery and heard the sounds of ships grinding against the sandy beaches. But all they could see were the ominous dragon heads glaring up at them.

Ruins at Lindisfarne.
https://pixabay.com/photos/ruins-lindisfarne-priory-lindisfarne-2021105/

But then they saw the Vikings surging from the ships. Battle cries roared from the brawny warriors as they swarmed the monastery. Monks scattered and hid but to no avail. Many religious community members were massacred during the attack. Some were taken as prisoners. Before the Vikings returned to their ships, they pillaged St. Cuthbert's Church and the priory. Ransacking and looting resulted in treasures of gold and silver religious relics. Embroidered silken vestments and embellished manuscripts were also seized by the invaders.

The unexpectedness and brutality of the raid alarmed and outraged the Christian world. The Holy Island was an especially important and symbolic location for the early Christians. St. Aidan founded the priory at Lindisfarne in 635. From there, the teachings of the church spread. St. Cuthbert was buried at this site, which added to the importance of its role in the church. Cuthbert was considered the patron saint of Northumbria and had served as the bishop of the abbey. Known for performing miracles as a healer, Cuthbert was revered by Christians. His grave was not destroyed in the raid, and his body was subsequently moved from the island.

The Holy Island also held another treasure of the early church: the Lindisfarne Gospels. Eadfrith, a bishop of the priory, spent at least five years creating this medieval manuscript. The Lindisfarne Gospels were filled with stunning illustrations and impeccable calligraphy. Thankfully, these gospels survived the 793 raid. However, its gem-studded cover did not; speculation is that the cover was stolen during the looting.

Since the Lindisfarne Monastery contained such a wealth of treasures and had such a rich history, it was able to survive and continue its mission until 875. At that time, the monks left the monastery because of the continuous threat of Viking incursions.

For this being the Vikings' first organized pillage, they were incredibly successful. Obtaining silver and gold was one of their probable motivating factors, and they surely obtained this wealth during the raid. This new wealth enabled the Vikings returning home to obtain a new status in their society. Those who participated in the raid had the resources to buy their own farmland, which improved their ranking. It also provided an incentive for others to join upcoming raids. Another aspect of participating in the raid was gaining a prestigious reputation as a Viking warrior.

Viking raids on monasteries continued for the next few summers, after which the number and intensity of the incursions grew. Places of worship were not selected because the Vikings were pagans; they tended to target remote sanctuaries. Often, the inhabitants, mainly monks and other religious people, were not armed, which made the looting and capturing of people to enslave easier to accomplish. Monasteries also contained portable treasures. Articles used as part of the liturgy and for worship were made from coveted metals.

The earliest Viking raids sailed from Norway. The early locations of the Norwegian Vikings were situated along the northeast shoreline of England. After the attack on Lindisfarne, the next year, in 794, the twin monasteries of Monkwearmouth-Jarrow were raided, resulting in destruction and looting. The following year, the Vikings pillaged and ransacked St. Columba on Iona. Vikings stole crosses, liturgical garments, chalices, candlesticks, and other portable riches from these religious establishments.

As more Scandinavian countries entered the Viking Age and joined in the pursuit of wealth and power, the attacks grew beyond monasteries. In the next century, the Vikings conquered parts of England and broadened their scope to northern Europe, Iceland, and Greenland.

Chapter 3: Viking Conquests

In the 800s, Vikings from across Scandinavia participated in raids. Norwegian Vikings tended to attack Ireland, Scotland, and northwest England. The Danes overlapped the Norwegians in England, but they also sailed to the Netherlands and France. Russia and areas to the east and south were targeted by the Swedish Vikings.

In the early 9th century, Viking raids continued. They followed a pattern similar to what had been inflicted upon Lindisfarne and other monasteries at the end of the 8th century. Throughout the 9th century, the intensity and scope of the raids increased. By the mid-9th century, the raiding Vikings began successfully invading and controlling countries. The Vikings established themselves in many countries. They built forts that were used as centers from which they organized their attacks. Also, by the middle of the 9th century, there is evidence of overwintering, which means the Vikings stayed through the winter.

Many famous and infamous leaders and warriors emerged throughout the age of Viking conquests. Viking incursions had lasting ramifications. The era's impacts spread from the shores of North America to Greenland, Paris, Istanbul (Constantinople), and Kyiv (Kiev). England, especially Northumbria, endured the most attacks.

Map of the Kingdom of Northumbria.
Hogweard, CC BY-SA 4.0 <https://creativecommons.org/licenses/by-sa/4.0>, via Wikimedia Commons; https://commons.wikimedia.org/wiki/File:Map_of_the_Kingdom_of_Northumbria_around_700_AD.svg

Ragnar Lothbrok or Lodbrok, who raided in the 9th century, was the embodiment of a Viking warrior. Fantastical stories abound detailing his larger-than-life accomplishments. Some of the claims are so extraordinary that there has been speculation about the veracity of Ragnar being one person. Perhaps some of the stories about Ragnar are about Ragnall, a composite of people, or a mythical figure. Many agree that there is sufficient evidence that supports the exploits of Ragnar since he is referenced in the *Anglo-Saxon Chronicle*.

Those living in England, Ireland, and France in the mid-9th century feared the fabled warrior. Ragnar altered the tactics of the raiders who preceded him. In addition to looting, it is believed that Ragnar was the first Viking raider who sought to control land and build settlements.

A skilled seaman, Ragnar sailed his fleet of longships on the rivers deep into current-day France. These ships were able to navigate the shallower waters. This design increased the scope of areas the Vikings could attack. They no longer needed to hover in the ocean waters close to the shore. Surprise attacks on European cities increased, many of them led by Ragnar. Fear of the Vikings spread throughout Europe, with Viking technology and shipbuilding adding to the prowess of the warriors.

Vikings first attacked the Frankish Empire in 799. The raids grew in frequency and scope in the subsequent years. After Charlemagne's death in 814, there were internal struggles for control of the vast empire. The Vikings were aware of the power void and planned their raids accordingly. The Frankish Empire suffered at least five significant raids before the siege of Paris in 845. After one of the incursions, Ragnar was granted land by the king. Over time, the king and Ragnar had a falling out, so Ragnar had his land taken away. On his way up the Seine to Paris, Ragnar and his men exacted their revenge and plundered Rouen.

After propelling his fleet of 120 ships and over 5,000 warriors on the Seine River, the siege of Paris commenced. This was Ragnar's and the Vikings' largest assault on the Frankish Empire. Aware of the assault and in an attempt to protect the Abbey of Saint-Denis, King Charles the Bald (Charles II) separated his army into two divisions, stationing them on each side of the river.

In response, Ragnar attacked and routed the army located on one side of the Seine. The Vikings paid homage to their god Odin. To send a message to the king and his remaining troops, the Vikings captured over one hundred soldiers. Then the enemy combatants were hanged and displayed on an island situated in the Seine.

Ragnar and his warriors refused to leave Paris until they received over seven thousand pounds of silver and gold from King Charles the Bald. It is believed that the payment partly reimbursed Ragnar for the land Charles had taken back from him. This is the first known payment to the Vikings to withdraw from a land that they invaded. The Vikings would receive at least twelve more such payments, which are referred to as Danegeld.

Ragnar followed the agreement and departed from Paris as soon as he was paid. However, as he and his warriors sailed back down the Seine, they looted many towns and monasteries. Ragnar's raiding adventures did not conclude with Paris. He continued pillaging areas of England and Ireland.

The actual cause of Ragnar's death is not certain. Legends tell of the king of Northumbria throwing Ragnar into a pit of venomous snakes. Evidence does not fully substantiate the tale, nor is there proof that Ragnar's sons attacked England to avenge their father's death. However, Ragnar's legacy grew through the plundering wrecked upon England by his sons.

Inwaer or Ivar the Boneless, Halfdan, Björn Ironside, Sigurd Snake-in-the Eye, Hvitserk, and Ubba are the sons of Ragnar who led or were related to the Great Heathen Army. The legend associated with their invasion of England centers on their seeking revenge against King Ælla. Once the Viking warriors captured the king, the brothers allegedly performed a blood eagle ritual on him.

Using sharp weapons, the tormentors sliced open the back of the still-living victim, King Ælla. Then his ribs were cleaved from his spine. The captors next pulled the king's ribs through the opening to create the shape of wings. Lastly, the victim's two fully intact lungs were dragged out of his body. The lungs would have been placed on the ribs to complete the creation of an eagle. Researchers into this horrific practice believe the victim was dead by the time the lungs were removed.

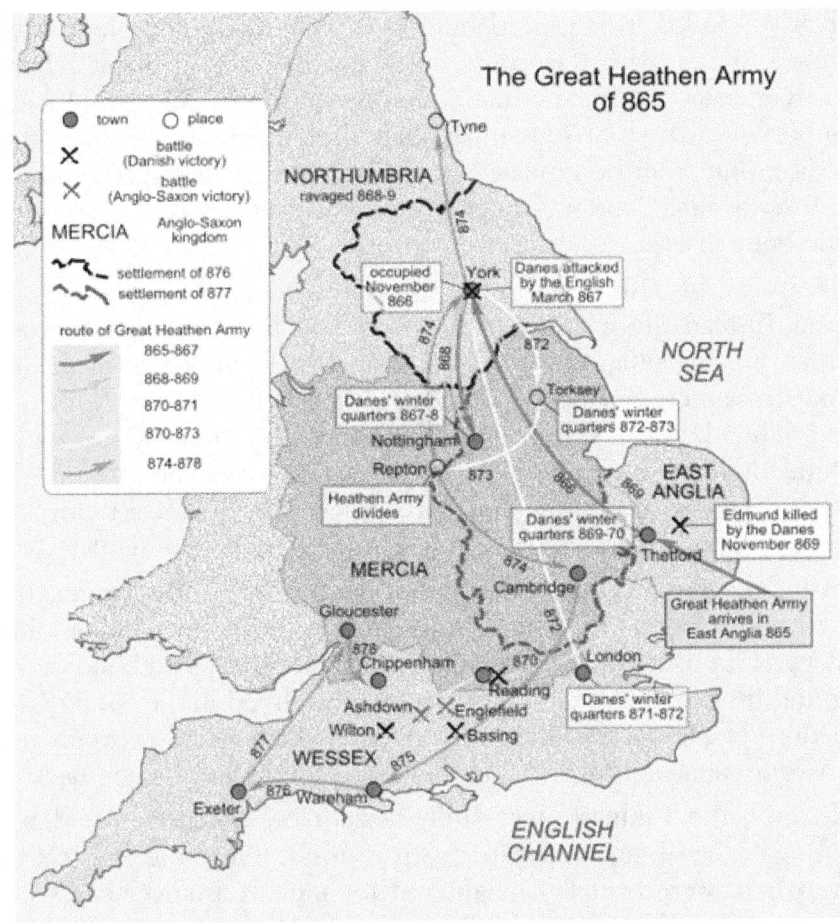

Map tracking the advances of the Great Heathen Army.
Hel-hama, CC BY-SA 3.0 <https://creativecommons.org/licenses/by-sa/3.0>, via Wikimedia Commons; https://commons.wikimedia.org/wiki/File:England_Great_Army_map.svg

Regardless of the brothers' actual motivation to invade England, the Great Heathen Army (also known as the Great Viking Army) stormed England in 865. It is not certain if all the brothers led the forces, but there is evidence to support that Ivar the Boneless and Björn Ironside were members and leaders of the formidable army.

Estimates of the army range from over one thousand fighters to thousands of Vikings from a coalition of Scandinavian forces. The army attacked England when they disembarked on the shores of East Anglia. Unlike other invasions, this force sought more than loot. The Great Heathen Army undertook the goal of conquering and controlling England.

Ivar's moniker as Ivar the Boneless is presumed to be the result of a curse. Aslaug, who was Ivar's mother and a Norse oracle, shared with Ragnar a vision she had. Before marrying Ragnar, Aslaug's prophecy told her that she and Ragnar should not consummate their marriage until after he returned from raiding. Ragnar did not listen to her forewarning. Ivar was born with what is thought to have been brittle bone disease.

However, his affliction did not soften Ivar's bloodthirsty quests as a Viking. Instead, stories were told of how Ivar Ragnarsson battled as a berserker. This subgroup of Viking warriors, berserkers, fought in a frenzied manner. Berserkers dedicated their battles to the Norse god Odin. They believed the bear's spirit joined their bodies and minds, making them invulnerable. Some berserkers wore bear skins into battle; others wore nothing and bared their skin. Their screams and intensity made berserkers beyond fearsome to their opponents.

After the Great Heathen Army's conquest of Northumbria, they gained control of York, which culminated with the devastating killing of King Ælla. But Ivar coveted all of England. On his path to control, Ivar and his men left death, destruction, and dread in their wake. The Kingdom of Mercia was their most difficult challenge. For over a year, the Vikings attacked Mercia, but they were continually beaten back.

In 869, the Vikings successfully seized the Kingdom of Mercia. Those who had fought against Ivar from inside the protective walls of Nottingham were brutally slaughtered for their resistance. Ivar's next target was King Edmund and East Anglia.

Edmund futilely led his forces against the Great Heathen Army. Some legends tell of Ivar and his invaders capturing the king. Ivar's violent killing of Edmund garnered the king the status of martyr and sainthood. Ivar had the king tied to a tree in the village of Hoxne. Edmund was savagely beaten with clubs because he refused to recant his Christian beliefs. Then the Vikings shot Edmund until his body was filled with arrows. Finally, Ivar permitted the king to die. Once King Edmund was dead, the Vikings beheaded him. As a sign of disrespect, Ivar had his men discard Edmund's body and head into nearby thorn bushes.

The Vikings massacred other survivors and plundered homes and monasteries. Ivar controlled Britain and Ireland. Ivar continued his destructive ways until his death in 873. The leadership of the Great

Heathen Army was passed to Ivar's brothers, who were also sons of Ragnar.

Image of Erik the Red.
https://commons.wikimedia.org/wiki/File:Eric_the_Red.png

Ragnar Lothbrok's family was not the only one set on exploring. Naddodd was distantly related to Erik the Red on his father's side. Naddodd sailed from Norway with the goal of settling on the Faroe Islands in the first part of the 9th century. However, he and his crew lost their way at sea and landed on the east coast of present-day Iceland. The men did not encounter any signs of human life after exploring the land and eventually returned to Norway. Naddodd shared his story, and soon others set sail to explore Iceland, although credit for discovering the land was bestowed upon Naddodd.

A few generations later, Naddodd's distant relation, Thorvald Ásvaldsson, sailed from Norway to Iceland. However, Thorvald's purpose was not to seek the Faroe Islands and sail off-course. Thorvald was banished from Norway around 960 by King Haakon the

Good because of transgressions that included multiple killings. Found guilty of manslaughter, Thorvald took his family, which included his son, Erik the Red, with him to serve his sentence in Iceland.

The family lived in the wilds of western Iceland. In time, Erik Thorvaldsson (better known as Erik the Red) became infamous as a Viking with a proclivity for exploring. He was also known for having an explosive disposition like his father. With his fiery red hair and beard and a temper to match, Erik the Red was feared by many.

Erik's marriage to the well-to-do Thjodhild Jörundsdóttir enhanced his role as a leader in the community. His wife's wealth included a number of thralls or enslaved people that added to their status, which Erik received as part of the marriage. Erik's neighbor, Valthjof, lost his house in a landslide. The devastation was blamed on Erik's newly acquired thralls.

In retaliation, all of Erik's thralls were butchered by Eyiolf the Foul, a relative or friend of Valthjof. Erik took the law into his own hands, refusing to wait until the ruling council or Althing gathered. He responded by slaughtering Eyiolf the Foul and Holmgang-Hrafn, the latter of whom was involved in the murder of his thralls. Relatives of the Valthjof clan were outraged. Erik the Red and his family were expelled from the community. Like father, like son.

Erik and his family moved to the island of Oxney, which was not any more peaceful for them. Erik had possession of *setstokkrs*. These massive beams were inscribed with runic Norse pagan symbols that conveyed religious symbolism. Care of the *setstokkrs* was given to Thorgest, Erik's neighbor. However, when Erik wanted the beams returned to him, Thorgest refused. Again, instead of seeking assistance from the local council, Erik reclaimed the beams by force. In the melee, two of Thorgest's sons were killed.

The village council debated what punishment should be inflicted on Erik. For his murderous ways, Erik the Red was again banished from the community. For three years, Erik was not permitted to live in Oxney or any part of Iceland. Tired of the rules of the Viking communities in Iceland, Erik set sail.

A hundred years earlier, a Norwegian, Gunnbjörn Ulfsson, had encountered a large piece of land, a fact Erik knew. Erik sailed over nine hundred miles and is credited as the leader of the first group that settled what is today Greenland. They established their community at a fjord called Tunulliarfik. For the rest of his exile, Erik explored and mapped out Greenland. At the end of his banishment, Erik returned to Iceland, seeking to encourage others to join him in the icy tundra that he named Greenland, which he named in the hopes of attracting more settlers.

Erik the Red's children continued with their father's love of navigation and exploration. His daughter, Freydis, had a similar temperament as him. Leif Eriksson is known for being the first European to reach the shores of North America. About fifteen years before Leif sailed with a crew of about thirty-five men, North America had been sighted by Bjarni Herjólfsson when he sailed off-course.

Statue of Leif Eriksson.
Sharon Mollerus, CC BY 2.0 <https://creativecommons.org/licenses/by/2.0>, via Wikimedia Commons; https://commons.wikimedia.org/wiki/File:Leif_Erikson_Statue,_Duluth_(15290644106).jpg

Using that information, Leif's expedition landed in Newfoundland, where he established his base camp. Other excursions followed. His brother, Thorvald, and his crew lived in Vinland ("Land of Wine," with the name coming from the land's grapes) for at least two years. Thorvald was killed in a battle with the indigenous people of the area, making him the first European to die in North America. Thorstein, the third of Erik's sons, attempted to recover Thorvald's body.

However, storms prevented him from doing so.

Seeking the riches the land had to offer, the last Viking male from Greenland to lead an expedition to North America was Thorfinn Karlsefni. Their settlement lasted for about three years until trading with the indigenous people was no longer peaceful.

The last voyage to Vinland was led by Freydis, Erik the Red's daughter, was the last voyage to Vinland. Legends tell of Freydis sailing in partnership with Icelandic traders and their crews. Other stories tell of her sailing with her husband and his brothers. The Vikings sought grapes from the incredible vineyards and wood from the lavish forests. Regardless of the men with whom she sailed, Freydis was much like her father. She was cold-hearted and ruthless.

Legends abound about Freydis. One is that after she gathered what she wanted from the land, she had her crew chief murder all the men they did not need to sail back with. None of her men would kill the women, so Freydis did that herself. She threatened her crew with death if they ever shared the story of what happened in Vinland. Eventually, the story was revealed. However, she was not banished, but Freydis and her family were never truly accepted after the truth came out.

The Vikings never sailed to Vinland again. It is presumed that the distance, over 2,200 miles, was too difficult to traverse. Many of the same riches that Vinland offered could be found in Norway. Greenland also lacked sufficient people to sustain villages in North America, especially due to the distance and run-ins with the indigenous people.

Chapter 4: The Fall of the Vikings

From the explosive start of the Viking Age with the ravaging of Lindisfarne Monastery in 793 until 1066 with the Battle of Stamford Bridge, the appearance of a longboat sent shockwaves through villages and towns. As with the proliferation of Viking raids, the cessation of raids happened more gradually than ending dramatically in a final battle. The people who are referred to as Vikings existed before and after 793 and 1066.

Map of Viking expansion.
https://commons.wikimedia.org/wiki/File:Viking_Expansion.svg

Most of the people who inhabited modern-day Scandinavia never sailed on a longboat or participated in raids. Thus, the end of the Viking Age did not equate to the annihilation of them as a people. However, the days of raiding, exploring, and pillaging faded away in the 11th century. Many evolving factors contributed to the demise of the Vikings as a band of warriors.

Under the leadership of Cnut the Great, also spelled Canute and Knut, the first stages of the changing landscape of the Viking raids occurred. As a young man, Cnut actively participated in Viking raids under the guidance of his father, Sweyn or Svein Forkbeard. Sweyn's style of raiding differed from the earlier raids of the 8th and early part of the 9th centuries. He was not content to just pillage monasteries; his raids had broader goals.

Sweyn's violent raids decimated much of England. Their king, Æthelred, paid Sweyn Danegeld, which was a type of extortion. Once the Vikings were paid the money, they were expected to leave. The larger forces complied, but smaller raiding parties continued to pillage the northern sections of England. In retaliation, Æthelred ordered the slaughter of all Danes in England.

A massacre on St. Brice's Day in 1002 killed Sweyn's sister. In a brutal response, Sweyn's forces invaded England the following year. Ruthless attacks were conducted by the invaders. For years, the battles raged back and forth between the English (then known as Anglo-Saxons) and Vikings. Again, King Æthelred resorted to paying Sweyn to leave England.

The raids subsided but did not conclude until 1013 when the lords and nobles of England conceded. They declared Sweyn king of England and forced Æthelred into exile. Sweyn became the first Viking king of England, adding another territory to his control (he was king of Denmark and Norway as well). This newly formed kingdom, referred to by historians as either the Anglo-Scandinavian or North Sea Empire, was short-lived, lasting for only about thirty years. Sweyn would only rule for about five weeks.

After Sweyn's death in 1014, Æthelred emerged from exile. With the support of England's nobles, Æthelred reestablished his kingdom. This forced the Viking army led by Cnut to leave English soil. However, Cnut regrouped his army and invaded England. By 1016, Cnut controlled much of England. London was ruled by Edmund,

Æthelred's son. Once Edmund died in November 1016, Cnut assumed control of all of England.

Cnut gained control of Denmark in 1019, and Norway fell under his leadership in 1028. Cnut was ruthless in his quest for power and control. During the first few years of his reign, Cnut ruled through fear. However, he grew to become a great leader.

Cnut was the first king to rule all of England since the days of the Roman Empire. He successfully led his kingdoms because he blended diverse cultures and people in his courts. He recognized and rewarded those who had supported him in England, Denmark, and Norway. His unification of these lands under his rule changed the course of history for the Vikings.

Map of Cnut's realm.
Soerfm, CC BY-SA 4.0 <https://creativecommons.org/licenses/by-sa/4.0>, via Wikimedia Commons; https://commons.wikimedia.org/wiki/File:Cnut-north-sea-empire.png

It did not benefit Cnut or his kingdoms for the Vikings to loot and raid England any longer. Cnut successfully set up trade routes that benefited all in the North Sea Empire. The infrastructures in his different domains were vastly improved. The people in his kingdoms flourished. At the time of his death in 1035, England, Denmark,

Norway, and parts of Sweden were stable.

Other areas in Europe also experienced different styles of leadership. This was another component that dramatically impacted the Vikings and their ability to successfully raid other countries. In part, the surge and power of the Vikings led to the restructuring of European governments.

Some leaders, such as Charlemagne, attempted to unite smaller kingdoms into larger ones under a central leadership. Charlemagne ruled over the Holy Roman Empire. However, those efforts largely collapsed after his death. The vacuum of unified leadership after the demise of the Holy Roman Empire allowed the Vikings to strike and loot lands more easily.

Gradually, Europe's system of government and its supporting military changed partly to meet the continual menace of the Viking raids. Feudalism was one of the negative factors that led to the end of the Viking Age, but this structure of ruling arose to address the rampage of the Vikings.

During the Early Middle Ages, Europe was not delineated like it is today, with defined countries or borders. Boundaries between kingdoms were often blurred. Centralized leadership, if it existed, was not able to defend or protect the entire kingdom. Without formal standing armies or militias, towns, villages, and monasteries had to find a way to defend themselves. The king's inability to effectively protect his kingdom gave rise to the hierarchical system of feudalism.

The local control of areas evolved into a system in which local lords or nobles ruled the land. On the top rung were the kings and queens. Royalty controlled all the land in the kingdom. However, the king and queen could not protect the vast lands that they ruled. In exchange for protecting the land and for loyalty, the king and queen allocated sections or units of land called a fief to a noble or lord.

The noble or lord ruled their fiefdom. In return for the land, the nobles became vassals of the king and queen, which meant they owed them their loyalty. Part of their allegiance to the crown was a pledge to protect the royal family.

Knights comprised the next tier of the system. Nobles or lords gave a section of their land to knights. Other compensation instead of land happened and could include money, housing, or equipment needed to perform their military obligations. In return, the knights were obligated to protect the nobles. The knights were trained in military operations and were called upon to fight any wars that the nobles or king and queen needed them for. Guarding the castle or providing a safe escort for the nobles and royalty also fell under the duties of the knights.

Surviving on the lowest rungs of the feudal society ladder were the peasants and serfs. Since peasants had mobility and could own land, they ranked above the serfs. Serfs were tied to the land and were comparable to thralls, although serfs had more rights. Tilling the land and providing products were the roles performed by the serfs. In exchange for their work in the fields, serfs were protected by the lord's militia.

This intricate system bonded each tier of society to each other. Dividing vast kingdoms into manageable sections that were controlled locally provided protection from the Vikings. Militias were formed and trained so they could defend their lands and people. In other areas, towns were moved away from the borders of rivers and oceans. Monasteries were relocated or built towers in which valuables could be hidden and defenses could be mounted. European towns and villages were no longer easy targets for the longships. For the Vikings, these obstacles reduced the profitability and ease of the raids.

Transformations within the Viking homelands also impacted Viking explorers and their ability to successfully continue their raiding and expansion. Similar to the rest of Europe, the boundary lines of Scandinavian countries continued to shift throughout the 11th century. During this period, Denmark, Sweden, and Norway began evolving to become separate kingdoms. As Scandinavian kings unified their lands, the culture of participating in Viking raids began to lose support.

Society at the beginning of the Viking Age was not as hierarchal as the feudal system that began to expand throughout Europe. Early raiders were often young male farmers who traveled for adventure and wealth. Upon their return, the former raiders would settle on their farms and have a family. With more centralized governments forming in the Scandinavian lands and a developing stratification of society, these young men no longer had the freedom to join the raids.

The date used by many as the fall of the Vikings was the Battle of Stamford Bridge. This battle was another contributing factor to the demise of the Vikings. After Cnut's death, his son, Harold Harefoot, became king of England. His reign was short-lived, and he died less than five years after assuming the throne. Another of Cnut's sons, Harthacnut, was named king; his tenure lasted a little over two years before his death. Before he died, Harthacnut named Edward the Confessor, son of King Æthelred, to be his successor. In 1042, Edward the Confessor became king of England.

And then things got complicated. When Edward died in 1066, he did not have a direct heir, which resulted in a dispute over who should succeed him. Three leading claimants felt they had valid rights to his throne. Promises were made to some; family connections made others viable candidates, and politics put other successors in contention. One contender was Harold Godwinson, the earl of Wessex, who was Edward's brother-in-law. William of Normandy was Edward's first cousin. And lastly, there was Edgar, the son of Edward the Exile, who was in the family bloodline but was very young.

The Battle of Hastings eventually resolved the dispute between Harold Godwinson and William of Normandy. It is uncertain if Edward the Confessor had a preference for who should succeed him. However, before that final showdown, there was a complication with another contender, Harald Hardrada, who was the king of Norway and the descendant of King Cnut. Joining and encouraging Harald Hardrada in his pursuit of England's crown was Tostig Godwinson, Harold's brother, who had been exiled by his brother and was looking to regain power. In 1066, King Harald Hardrada and Tostig led an armada of three hundred ships filled with over ten thousand warriors. On their way to battle with King Harold, the Vikings successfully fought Edwin and Morcar, the earls of Mercia and Northumbria, respectively.

Overconfident due to their recent successes, the Vikings were not fully prepared for battle. At the Battle of Stamford Bridge, both Tostig and Harald were killed. The Vikings were decimated. There were so few survivors that the Vikings needed only twenty-four of the three hundred ships they used to sail to England.

King Harold of England and his troops greatly diminished the Vikings' ability to continue inflicting their reign of terror. However, Harold's victory was fleeting in part because of the Vikings' initial successes in the Battle of Stamford Bridge.

Another leader of Viking descent also claimed that he was the legitimate king of England. William the Conqueror, who was a distant relation of Rollo, who became the first ruler of Normandy, claimed that his cousin, King Edward the Confessor, promised him the throne. William and his forces from Normandy invaded England in response to Harold not acknowledging his claims. In the Battle of Hastings, the Norman troops killed King Harold Godwinson and defeated the English troops in October 1066. William was crowned king of England on Christmas Day, 1066.

After gaining the kingship, William faced numerous battles and challenges to his leadership before he conquered all of England. William sought complete control over England to protect his new kingdom from invasions, and he handily defeated his opponents. One of his last conquests was against King Sweyn II of Denmark.

This last Viking incursion began in 1069. English forces opposed to William requested King Sweyn's assistance. The Danish king sent his Vikings under the charge of his sons and brother, Asbjørn, to unite with Prince Edgar Ætheling, Æthelred II's great-grandson, and attack the coast of England and the town of York. They were temporarily successful in their capture of York; however, once William and his forces arrived on the scene, the rebels and Vikings were driven out. Still, the Vikings fled with the treasures they pillaged.

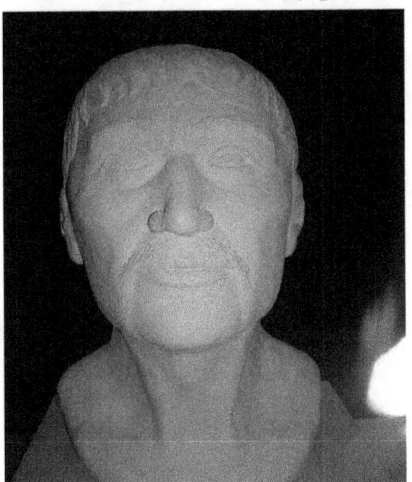

Statue of King Sweyn II.
Arne Kvitrud, CC BY-SA 4.0 <https://creativecommons.org/licenses/by-sa/4.0>, via Wikimedia Commons;https://commons.wikimedia.org/wiki/File:Svein_Estridssons_hode.JPG

In an attempt to keep the Vikings from returning, William was compelled to pay them and resorted to Danegeld. They stayed over the winter until reinforcements arrived, led by King Sweyn II. The Vikings joined forces with another rebel Anglo-Saxon leader, Hereward. Following Viking norms, they raided Peterborough Abbey. Knowing they would not defeat William, the Vikings took their treasures and set sail.

Longships would no longer suddenly appear on the shores of monasteries seeking gold and treasures as they did before. Vikings assimilated back into their homelands as farmers and craftsmen. Raids were no longer profitable due to the changing dynamics of societal structures and norms in Scandinavian and European countries.

PART TWO: Regular Viking Life

Chapter 5: Societal Structure

The majority of those who lived during the Viking Age did not participate in raids. During this era, most people lived in towns and villages in Scandinavia. Warriors who did take part in pillaging returned home to their families. Their structured world has been pieced together from evidence discovered by archaeologists and other societies that wrote about the Vikings.

In many depictions of this world, there were four separate tiers. At the top of the pyramid were members of royalty, kings, and queens. This class emerged as a more powerful group as the Viking Age progressed.

Nobles and jarls formed the next class in society. Within this grouping were chieftains and military leaders who owned large estates. Jarls frequently recruited their own militia to protect their land. To foster loyalty, jarls hosted lavish feasts and festivals to honor gods and celebrate military victories and successful harvests.

The majority of the Viking era population belonged to the karls or freemen. Tradesmen, craftsmen, skilled workers, and farmers made up this group. This group, with its skilled boat builders, was essential to the success of the Viking raids. The Viking society's fourth class included slaves or thralls, who performed the most difficult work on the farms. Without thralls, farms would not have survived.

One was born into their class; however, there was some mobility to move up or down based on one's contributions or lack of to society. For example, if a jarl lost his land or wealth, he would become a karl.

To protect one's status in society, many people were willing to fight to retain their class level. Violence was also inflicted on people who did not demonstrate the proper respect for someone of a higher societal level.

The structure of Viking society can be found in an ancient myth. In the poem *Rígsthula*, the Scandinavians talked about the classes. As with many stories from so long ago, there are different versions. In some depictions, Ríg and his descendants formed a four-tiered society; in other iterations, Ríg created a world with three classifications.

The god Heimdall disguised himself as Ríg and traveled to this world, which was also called Midgard or Middle Earth. During his time on Earth, Ríg stayed with three different families for three nights. While visiting, Ríg slept between each family's heads of the household. From these liaisons, a number of children were conceived. These children were the ancestors of each class of society.

Ríg in great-grandfather's cottage.
https://commons.wikimedia.org/wiki/File:Rig_in_Great-grandfather%27s_Cottage.jpg

Ríg's first stop on Middle Earth was an impoverished couple, Ái (great-grandfather) and Edda (great-grandmother). Though they were poor, the couple shared with Ríg their meager dwelling and food. Nine months after Ríg's visit, Edda gave birth to Thrall, which is believed to mean "Slave." He performed some of the more labor-intensive tasks on Ái's and Edda's land. Later on, Thrall met and had children with Thír. Thrall, Thír, and their children were all physically unkempt. They all performed tasks that required manual labor.

After Ríg's first stop on Middle Earth, he met Afi (grandfather) and Amma (grandmother). This couple lived in a modest but clean farmhouse. As with his first visit, Ríg stayed for three days and nights. Each night, he slept between Afi and Amma. Karl, which means freeman, was born to Amma nine months after Ríg stayed with the couple. Karl helped Afi and Amma on the farm. He married Snør (daughter-in-law), with whom he had children from whom farmers descended.

For his last visit, Ríg stopped at a large home that was beautifully decorated. He was invited to dine with Fadir (father) and Módir (mother). They treated Ríg to lavish feasts. Ríg slept nightly between Fadir and Módir. Nine months later, Jarl (earl) was born. Jarl learned how to communicate with runes, make and use weapons, and successfully fight in wars. Due to his prowess as a warrior, Jarl was rewarded with the ownership of eighteen farms.

Jarl married Erna, with whom he fathered several children. His youngest son, Konr (king), was the ancestor of Viking royalty. Ríg's time on Midgard provided the tiers of Viking society. He fathered three sons who each started the lineage of the class of thralls, karls, and jarls. His grandson, Konr, was the first king of the Norse lands.

Kings were not selected based on their bloodlines, nor were they a powerful force at the beginning of the Viking Age. Throughout the era of the Vikings, the countries of Denmark, Norway, and Sweden emerged as separate entities. With that evolving structure, the role of kings and queens also transitioned.

During the Viking Age, Norse royalty was expected to be brave, exhibit leadership, and be fierce warriors. Most Viking kings were selected from local chieftains. They were chosen based on their accomplishments. Wealth also contributed to their power, as chieftains were able to finance more men for their army. The ability to create and retain bonds of loyalty was important for chieftains to maintain their role and be elevated to royalty.

Allegiance to the king or chieftain was also important. Without loyalty, it was difficult for a leader to provide protection for his kingdom. The area over which a king ruled in the Viking Age does not correspond to modern-day boundaries for any of the Scandinavian countries. The domains kings ruled over were compilations of small kingdoms and various chiefdoms. His ability to stay in power necessitated frequent battles with other local leaders.

As the Viking Age and the reach of the Vikings grew, the role of royalty changed. Kings became leaders of larger and larger swathes of land and people. With a more centralized power base, they were able to conscript more men to join the military. Since there was not a bloodline lineage of royalty at the beginning of the Viking Age, they relied heavily on the support of the people they ruled. Warriors' loyalty was often based on how much the king shared feasts, weapons, and mutual alliances with them. Leaders who were not generous with their riches were susceptible to being overthrown.

Due to their wealth and power, earls or jarls became an influential class in Viking society. Many kings emerged from this group. Jarls were often landowners, successful traders, or merchants. The jarls used similar methods as the kings, rewarding those who worked their lands with celebrations centered around food and drink. Jarls also shared treasures from Viking raids to ensure the loyalty of those living in their chiefdom. These powerful men did not just spoil the villagers to show their wealth; they expected allegiance from the freemen to join them in battles or on Viking raids.

Early on in the Viking Age, there were more jarls than kings. Controlling smaller estates was more manageable than large kingdoms. Additionally, when Vikings settled the new lands they conquered, these settlements were ruled by jarls. Powerful jarls sought to find lands they could rule while on raids. Once in charge of the lands they captured, the new leaders could impose rules that were important to them.

Neither the kings nor the jarls could stay in power without the support of the karls or freemen. This third tier of Viking society fought battles with the jarls as they sought to conquer neighboring land. They followed their jarls onto ships to participate in raids and settled the lands that were captured in other countries.

Most of the members of this class were farmers. The early days of raiding were planned around the planting and harvesting seasons because of this. On these pillaging expeditions, karls were expected to provide their own weaponry. Karls needed shields, spears, and axes. Unlike jarls, the karls were not trained in combat. Jarls also entered battled better equipped. Only the wealthy warriors had spears and protective garments to wear into battle.

Replica of a Viking era farm.
Mark Voigt, CC BY 3.0 <https://creativecommons.org/licenses/by/3.0>, via Wikimedia Commons; https://commons.wikimedia.org/wiki/File:The_Viking_Farm,_Avaldsnes_05.2010_-_panoramio_(1).jpg

Though the karls were freemen, they relied heavily on their local leaders. Either the jarls or kings provided protection for the karls. Additionally, the top two tiers of society also controlled the wealth. Shares from raids provided the karls with income, but that amount was determined by the leaders. Also, if kings or jarls needed to increase their revenue, they could control the amount of goods that merchants sold. They could also demand tribute or protection money to permit merchants and traders to enter their lands.

As freemen, karls were able to own their own land. If they could not afford to buy their land, karls could rent land from the kings or jarls. They could choose to live where they wanted. Karls could also choose whether to start their own family or business.

In return for their freedom, karls were expected to swear an oath to promise their commitment to the local jarl or king. This pledge had to be taken when a boy reached adulthood. This allegiance also meant the karls had to fight on behalf of the jarl. Anytime the jarl needed assistance on his farm for planting or harvesting, he could summon the karls to help. In return, the jarls would keep the karls safe. Karls paid taxes in silver or gave a portion of their harvest to pay for the jarls' support.

The last tier of Viking society consisted of people referred to as thralls or slaves. The basis of the word "thrall" is Old Norse from *þræll*, which refers to a person who lived in a state of servitude. It is believed that the word slave is rooted in Slavic because many Slavic people during the Middle Ages were captured and sold into slavery.

In Viking society, a person was a slave if they were born to parents who were slaves. A person could be sold into slavery as punishment for certain crimes. If a family became financially destitute, they could sell themselves to another family to be their thralls. Many people became slaves because they were captured during a battle between two jarls; the prisoners of the victorious jarl were sold as slaves. Lastly, prisoners of Viking warriors became slaves when they arrived in Scandinavia.

People in this tier of society were not able to own land and were forced to work for their owners. The success of a farm depended on the people who worked the land. Therefore, slaves were not usually mistreated in the Viking Age. Slaves were permitted to marry and have children. Most thralls were allowed to have their own possessions. Farmers sometimes let slaves work for themselves and make money. Sometimes, slaves could share the earnings from raids. Some Vikings freed slaves as a reward for their work, and other slaves were able to save enough money to buy their freedom.

Women were not identified as a separate tier in Viking society, but they did have important roles in ensuring the smooth operation of daily life. As with other cultures of the same time period, men were considered superior to women. Men were responsible for fighting in battles, joining raids and other expeditions, farming, and hunting. Women controlled the household. Though wives were not equal to their husbands, women had more freedom than their contemporaries. Norse women were permitted to own property in their own names. They could also share their husband's wealth. Though marriages were often arranged, a woman could seek a divorce.

In some households, women had thralls who helped with the daily tasks of running a home. Maintaining a house included all aspects of food preparation and serving the food. Women had to manage the inventory and preparation of food that was stored for consumption between growing seasons. Women also ensured the family had sufficient provisions for the long winter. Milking the cows and producing butter and cheese were part of their daily tasks. Women also had to spin and weave to create cloth; then, they had to shape the cloth into garments and sew clothing for everyone in the house.

When the men of the village left to go raiding, the women were in charge. Symbolically and publicly, a husband would hand his household keys to his wife before setting sail. All in the village were informed of who was responsible for the farm and house while he was away. If her husband died, she was fully in control of the farm or business.

Everyone, regardless of societal ranking, contributed to the success of the village. Even children participated and had daily chores to complete. Children did not attend school. Instead, they learned the skills they needed to survive as an adult and had their own families. Boys would spend time with their fathers learning how to farm, fight, and fish. If their father were a craftsman, the son would be taught that trade. Girls learned how to prepare and store food, make clothes, sew, spin wool, knit, and brew ale.

Chapter 6: Village Life

In areas where the Vikings settled after raids, they installed their societal foundations. Part of their world was the structure of their class system. The Vikings also had an organized village life. Framing the workings of their communities was their method of governance, which was so effective that the Scandinavians instituted their legal system in the areas they settled.

One key component of the Viking judicial system was an assembly called the Thing or Althing. Various iterations of the spelling of "Thing" can be found in different regions. All variants are from the Old Norse word þing, which refers to a governing body or assembly. Governments in parts of Scandinavia continue to be based on Things. Denmark's Folketing or People's Thing, Norway's Storting or Great Thing, and Iceland's Althing or General Thing guide each country today. Iceland's Althing was established in 930 and is the oldest national parliament still in existence.

Althing in Iceland.
https://commons.wikimedia.org/wiki/File:Law_speaker.jpg

Throughout Scandinavian lands, including Viking colonies, Things were held in each village or community. All freemen, including jarls, were expected to attend and participate in their area's Thing. If they were not able to attend, a representative was sent instead, or the freemen had to pay a fine. Women also attended their village assembly unless they were widowers. Those who worked or lived alone were not required to attend unless the agenda for the meeting included selecting a king or deciding a murderer's fate.

Assemblies were held twice a year and lasted for many days. As a communal event, Things were a much-anticipated social gathering. Craftsmen brought goods to sell. Barrels of ale and mead were made by the local brewmaster. Meetings were arranged to be near sources of water. Fields were accessible for animals to graze, and hunting and fishing supplied food for all attendees. Community members shared the latest news about their families, which often led to the arrangement of marriages. Alliances were strengthened or dissolved.

Though these assemblies had a festive air to them, their main purpose was to craft new laws and to determine the guilt or innocence of anyone accused of crimes. Anyone in the community could bring a grievance before the Thing. Local chieftains presided over these early democratic assemblies. The lawspeaker assisted him in deciding cases or situations presented to the assembly.

Though Vikings did not record their laws and write them down, they did have a set of agreed-upon rules and regulations that governed their society. A lawspeaker attended each Thing. The lawspeaker could recite all of the Viking laws from memory. He could also recall decisions made at previous meetings. Lawspeakers would provide this information to those in charge of deciding the fate of the accused. Neighbors and those attending the Thing could voice their concerns about the charges being discussed before the final decision was made. The comments by the public unofficially assisted in the decision-making process.

If the offender was found guilty, they were fined, made a partial outlaw, or completely outlawed. Partial outlaws were banished from society for no longer than three years. Anyone fully outlawed was exiled for life. In addition to having to leave their town or village, full outlaws lost all of their property, although their families were not always exiled along with them. No one was permitted to assist an outlaw. This punishment was considered a horrific feat.

The Things had no power to enforce the decisions that were made. However, each Viking was bound by a sense of duty to their community and typically did as was expected.

In addition to meting out justice, Things set tax rates for people in the community. They also made certain that each man in their jurisdictions was properly equipped with weapons to protect the villages. Things also voted for kings. Lastly, these assemblies created new laws if deemed necessary. At the conclusion of the meeting, the people's agreement was demonstrated by shaking and clanging their weapons (*vápnatak*).

Another way disputes were resolved was through a duel or *hólmganga*. Duels had extremely strict rules that were enforced and monitored by a referee. *Hólmgangas* could only be fought on a ten-foot square space of a cloak. Stepping off the cloak was viewed as a spineless act (a *nithing*). Swords and shields were the weapons of choice by duelers. The man with the most wounds at the end of the duel lost, and he had to pay the winner with silver. If one dueler died, the winner or survivor assumed control of all of his property. Most *hólmgangas* resulted in the death of one of the combatants.

Dueling was deemed illegal during the reign of King Cnut. As the role and power of the kings grew throughout the Viking Age, more legal decisions were centralized. Loyalty and honor were two important traits for Vikings. Most members of Scandinavian societies followed rules of conduct. The desire to be respected guided one's daily decisions.

Societal norms dictated the behavioral expectations of villagers during the Viking Age. This included standards of comportment for banquets and other events. Feasts were held to celebrate various occasions, such as weddings, funerals, festivals, and successful raids and harvests.

The sharing of one's bounty was important for those hosting any feast. The success of the feast due to the host's hospitality could elevate a person's status in society. Guests were seated according to their status in the town. A stranger or visitor to a feast was required to recite his family's lineage so it could be determined where they should be positioned at the table.

Seating for a feast in the king's great hall or the local farmer's table was not done by chance. Valued guests earned a seat next to or across from the host. Whether the host was the king or the head of the house, they sat in the seat of honor (*hásæti*). The lowest-ranking guest was assigned the seat farthest away from the host. Errors in seating could lead to angry exchanges if it were perceived that one was not respected by the host.

Regardless of the wealth of the person holding the feast, the celebrations were lavish affairs. Some feasts and festivals lasted for days. During that time, attendees ate and drank copious amounts of food and beverages. Mead and ale were consumed along with vegetables and meats from farms.

Farming was essential to the survival of the Vikings. Yes, farming supplied food for feasts, but successful farms and the storage of food were needed to sustain Vikings through the cold, dark winter months. Most Viking farmers were self-sufficient, meaning they raised enough livestock and grew enough crops to survive without outside help. They supplemented meat from the animals they raised with hunting and fishing.

The majority of people during the Viking Age were farmers. Everyone in the family participated in agricultural activities. Most farms had slaves who assisted with some of the more challenging daily tasks. Those who did not farm, such as blacksmiths, traded their goods and services for food.

The lack of fertile and level land made growing enough food to feed a family challenging. Long, dark, cold winters added to the complexities faced by the Scandinavians. Though the summers provided long sunny days, the summers were brief, and the growing season was short. Participating in Viking raids added income for some of the Scandinavian farmers. Others took advantage of captured land in areas with better conditions for farming and resettled in new countries.

In the early days of Viking raids, prosperous villages consisted of six to eight farms. These homesteads were separated from each other and the village center. Farms in less flourishing areas were not centered around a village; instead, they were isolated farmhouses. Often, farms had fences that identified the land boundaries of the farm. Within the fenced area was a longhouse, which was the dwelling of the family and the farm animals. Keeping the animals in the longhouse protected the valuable livestock during the frigid winters and added warmth to the family home. Food storage, the farmer's workshop, and farming utensils were also stored in the longhouse.

As farms grew, the longhouse remained the focal building of the family farm. However, other outbuildings were added over time. Workshops, stables, and barns were constructed. The longhouse transitioned to becoming the family home. Most family farms operated independently. Farmers grew their own food, made their own tools, and constructed their own buildings.

Reconstructed longhouse.
Sven Rosborn, CC BY 3.0 <https://creativecommons.org/licenses/by/3.0>, via Wikimedia Commons; https://commons.wikimedia.org/wiki/File:Viking_house_Ale_Sweden.jpg

Buildings were erected near sources of water. Structures were also located on higher ground to allow for better drainage. Situating buildings on an elevated site also provided the farmer and his family greater visibility. Not everyone who approached the farm was a welcome visitor, so the inhabitants had time to gather their weapons for protection. Signal fires were lit to warn nearby farms of dangerous situations or summon assistance. Everyone on the farm was expected to support and defend each other. Local chieftains and neighbors assisted one another.

Fields for grazing and growing crops surrounded the buildings located on the farm. The most important livestock was the cattle. Runic symbols and the word for cattle, the *Fehu* rune and *fé*, respectively, equate these animals to money and wealth. In order to plant crops, oxen were needed to plow the fields. A range of foods was produced from dairy cows, some of which could be made into foods that the Vikings stored and consumed throughout the winter. Cheese, butter, and *skyr* (a product similar to yogurt) sustained Vikings throughout the winter. Some dairy products were also used to preserve meat for winter consumption.

Another animal raised by many Viking farmers was the sheep. In addition to sheep being a food and milk source, their wool was used to create fabric and clothing. During the summer months, livestock was herded and driven to pastures located higher in the mountains. They roamed freely and fed on the fertile lands. Small stables and huts were built near the summer grazing lands.

Someone from the family farm or a farmhand stayed up in the highlands with the herds. They milked the cows and ewes. Milk was stored and transported to the main farm in skin sacks. Often, the herds from different farms mingled together. At the end of the summer season, the herds had to be separated by its farm. They were then driven back to the family farm for the winter. Usually, dairy cows were housed in a barn during the winter and fed hay. Otherwise, there was the potential for starvation if they were left outside.

Other farm animals raised on Scandinavian farms included goats, horses, pigs, chickens, and ducks. All of them required hay to sustain themselves throughout the winter. Hay was vital to Viking life. Laws were agreed upon that necessitated the growing and harvesting of enough hay to feed the animals. It was against Scandinavian law to let land on which hay was growing to decay and not be harvested before it rotted.

Replica of a Viking farm.
Mark Voigt, CC BY 3.0 <https://creativecommons.org/licenses/by/3.0>, via Wikimedia Commons; https://commons.wikimedia.org/wiki/File:The_Viking_Farm,_Avaldsnes_05.2010_-_panoramio_(1).jpg

Farmers were tasked with ensuring they had an adequate supply of hay for the winter. At the end of the harvest season, they inventoried their hay and livestock. If there was not enough hay to feed all the animals for the entire winter, the farmer slaughtered the weakest animals.

Grains were the most common crops. Barley, rye, and oats were ground into flour. Women made bread, which was preserved and stored for consumption during the winter. Grains were also used to make porridge, flatbreads, and ale. Flax was also grown on farms and used to make textiles.

Vegetables were sown in the spring and harvested in the late summer and early fall. During the harvest season, Vikings consumed freshly harvested vegetables. Some of the crops were saved for the winter; those vegetables were dried. Women and children also collected wild berries, herbs, and other plants. These greens and fruits were eaten during the summer and fall. Some were set aside and prepared for the winter via salting or drying.

The Norse people ate twice a day: the *dagmal*, or day meal, and the *nattmal*, or night meal. The food served at each meal was similar, although the time of the year greatly influenced the availability of food. Stewed vegetables, meats, and fish were the most common dishes and were served with mead or ale. Water was not often consumed because one risked illness or death due to unclean water. Food not consumed at the meal would have been stored in the coolest part of the house. The leftovers were reheated and re-served at the next family meal.

Vikings worked long, arduous hours. Therefore, they needed to eat foods high in calories and fat content so they had enough energy to complete their daily tasks. While the Vikings consumed food without the benefit of refrigeration, they were healthy. The remains of the Scandinavian people do not show they were lacking in vitamins or minerals.

Chapter 7: Literature and the Runic Alphabet

Vikings were industrious workers and made the most out of the land they farmed. During village and family feasts, Vikings entertained themselves with storytelling and sharing poetry. The long, dark winter provided time for families and villagers to perform maintenance on their homes and farms. Warriors practiced their skills for the next season of sailing and raiding.

Adults and children played a variety of games. The Scandinavians were a competitive group. *Hnefatafl*, which was similar to chess, could end up as a physical match. Many of their activities involved challenging each other in feats of cliff jumping or rock climbing. Swimming matches could lead to attempts to drown each other.

Though the Vikings enjoyed physical and aggressive activities, they also valued the skills of poetry and storytelling. These two skills framed the enjoyment of many feasts. The hosts of feasts served the best food they had. Guests were expected to wear their finest garments. Tables were set, and hand-embroidered tapestries were displayed on the walls. Even the dirt floors, which usually were strewn with trash, were covered with straw.

Meats were frequently roasted on the spit over an open fire or boiled. The people used all the parts of the animals. For instance, sausages were made from the organs and blood of animals. Women and thralls prepared fish in many ways, including pickled, smoked, and dried.

The host's daughter(s) and the family thralls served mead and ale to the guests. Many Vikings drank from horns, which could not be placed down until they were emptied. Inebriation was common during feasts and festivals. In this spirited setting, the *skáld* or poet performed stories. Sometimes, the poet would compose pieces to honor the cause for celebration.

Poets were important people in Viking society. Their ability to retell their culture's myths, heroic tales, and oral histories was valued, especially since poets emphasized the traits that were important in the warrior tradition. "Saga" is an Old Norse word for "saying." The stories shared by the poets were done in the oral tradition. Each generation passed its narratives to the next generation. Influential families from the Viking Age hired their own family *skáld*. It was the family poet's role to learn and memorize the family history to share with future generations. The reciting of the family saga was often embellished by the poet, and over time, more embellishments and accomplishments were added.

Later in the Middle Ages, these tales were collected and recorded. The main bodies of sagas were written well after the events occurred. Stories from the Viking Age are an intricate fusion of adventures and historical events that included the politics of the time. As with many tales written years later, they are a blend of fact and fiction. But with evidence from archaeological discoveries, some of the events, such as the Vikings sailing to North America, have been verified.

The *skálds* wove such incredible tales that their format influenced the development of prose in literature. Most literature committed to writing during the Middle Ages was poetry. But the Scandinavian tales were about everyday protagonists. Kings, queens, gods, and goddesses did not fill the pages of Scandinavian narratives.

The lead characters in the tales included shipbuilders, farmers, warriors, and others from everyday life. Sagas from the Norse focused on telling people's actual stories. The Norse sagas were categorized by genre, depending upon the topic of the narrative.

Stories about legendary or heroic figures are grouped as fornaldarsögur. Listeners would hear about people from the ancient past. Elements of fantasy were part of the plot line and included dragons, dangerous quests, and mythical creatures. Kings and queens were prominent in the stories known as konungasögur. In these stories, actual events framed the narrative, along with details about leaders from the time period. Another genre of sagas was family sagas or the Íslendingasögur. In these narratives, the stories and struggles of everyday people and the complexity of the human experience provided listeners with real role models.

Title page of the Prose Edda.
https://commons.wikimedia.org/wiki/File:Edda.jpg

Another grouping of stories based on the Scandinavian oral storytelling tradition is the Eddas. These collections tell of the gods and goddesses of the Viking world. There are two groups of Eddas. The *Elder Edda*, also called the *Poetic Edda*, is based on a document from the Middle Ages, the *Codex Regius*. The *Younger Edda*, which was also referred to as the *Prose Edda*, was written by Snorri Sturluson. Together, the *Poetic Edda* and the *Prose Edda* provide rich sources of Norse mythology and ancient belief systems from long ago. Materials in both Eddas were formed into manuscripts in the 13th century.

Works included in the *Poetic Edda* are tales from Norse myths. It is the most extensive written compilation of stories from the oral tradition of Scandinavian tales. Poems in the anthology tell of the Norse gods and the world's origins, as well as legends and heroes of the Viking world. Snorri Sturluson wrote the "newer" or *Younger Edda*. In this volume, Sturluson shared tales that show the beliefs and customs of the Scandinavian people. Stories of incredible warriors and their fantastic feats are available for today's readers, allowing them to access the Vikings' heroic past and other worlds.

Part of what influenced Sturluson to compose his text was the desire to preserve the poetic past of the Viking world. Poetry was used to memorialize incredible occurrences and the people involved. His textbook taught others how to continue creating skaldic poetry in the Scandinavian tradition. His work, sometimes referred to as *Snorra Edda*, provides information on myths from the Norse world, a guide to writing poetry, how the skaldic poets chose their words, and the rhythm schematics employed by the ancient poets.

The people of the Viking Age did not write manuscripts. Similar to the lawspeakers, who were responsible for memorizing laws, poets used verse as a means for ideas to be recalled and shared. This proved to be an effective method of communicating between distances and time. Poems and their messages ranged from words of praise and adulation to insults and vilification.

The words created by poets were so important that kings had their own poets as part of their entourage to memorialize their great deeds. Poets were key figures in Viking society. They held the power to preserve events and affect history. They also entertained at feasts and festivals. If a poet wrote a verse about a person, their accomplishments or misdeeds were recorded for all time. This either elevated or deflated one's status and their family's ranking in their community.

To enable poets to view events, kings created shield walls or *skjaldborgs*. Poets observed battles from a safe distance. They took notes and composed poems that retold the sequence of events and highlighted memorable deeds of warriors and leaders.

In addition to creating new verses, poets were also a source of past knowledge. Queries about past events, leaders, or families could be posed to a local poet, who was expected to be able to accurately answer any questions. Snorri Sturluson shared the details of how verses were expected to be formatted. The patterns of alliteration, rhythm, and internal rhyme served as cues for those reciting the poems. Intricacies in word choice and construction enabled the conveyors of information to recall numerous verses correctly.

Kings and leaders used poems to inspire warriors before battles. The creative fusions of words entertained people at royal and village feasts. Ordinary people were honored through artistic expression, while others were scorned for their actions by poets.

Another means of memorializing people and events was through words engraved on stone monuments. Messages written in runes were inscribed on a variety of materials for a number of distinct purposes. Unlike poems, which allowed for lengthy messages, runes were usually brief and concise. Similar to poets, a rune writer was viewed as having valuable skills that they learned and mastered.

Sixteen runes or characters comprised the basic Viking alphabet. Each letter was formed from a distinct sequence of lines. The various patterns of lines represented each of the sixteen letters. Sometimes, the runic alphabet is called Futhark, which is the first six letters (f, u, th, a, r, and k) of the full alphabet, which contains sixteen letters.

Lines were used to form letters since they could be easily chiseled into many different materials. Each glyph or symbol represented a sound. Each vertical line that was part of a letter was called a stave. Diagonal markings were called twigs. Horizontal lines were not used in the letters because they could be misconstrued as part of the woodgrain.

ᚠᚢᚦᛅᚱᚴ   ᚼᚾᛁᛏᛋ   ᛏᛒᛘᛦ
ᚠᚢᚦᚫᚱᚴ   ᚺᚾᛁᛄ'   ᛃᛖᛏᛚ,
fuþąrk hnias tbmlʀ

Image of runes.
https://commons.wikimedia.org/wiki/File:Yngre_futharken.svg

Runic inscriptions were used to communicate many different ideas in the Viking world. Some messages simply identified the owner of an object. Merchants and traders used rune sticks to track the selling and buying of goods. The costs were recorded, and the buyer of the goods or the seller of the merchandise was identified through the use of runes. Informational messages, love notes, and complaints were shared using runes. Due to the broad usage of runes, many historians believe the Vikings were fairly literate.

In addition to runes' uses for common, everyday notes and messages, they were also a means to memorialize the dead. Sometimes, these brief yet remarkable lines are classified as another category of Viking poetry. Elite families could have memorials with runic inscriptions that detailed the accomplishments of the deceased.

Two of the most well-known runestones are located in Jelling, Denmark. The older of the two stones, dating back to the 10th century, was raised by King Gorm the Old to honor his wife, Queen Thyre. One translation of the runes celebrating Queen Thyre acknowledges her as the savior of Denmark.

Picture of the Jelling runestones.
Alicudi, CC BY-SA 3.0 <https://creativecommons.org/licenses/by-sa/3.0>, via Wikimedia Commons; https://commons.wikimedia.org/wiki/File:Runesten_i_Jelling.jpg

It is believed that while King Gorm and other leaders were participating in Viking raids, Thyre led Denmark. To fight off Saxon invasions, the queen continued building the defensive Dannevirke. The construction of this protective wall began in the 6th century. The largest sections of Dannevirke were constructed during the Viking Age.

After King Gorm and Queen Thyre died, their son, Harald Blatand (better known as Harald Bluetooth), became ruler. He had a runestone constructed to pay tribute to his parents. A tribute to King Harald is also on the stone. Harald ruled both Denmark and Norway. Harald inscribed a portrayal of Jesus on the stone to acknowledge his role in bringing Christianity to Denmark. Both Jelling stones are now

UNESCO World Heritage Sites.

Part of King Harald Blatand's legacy was his ability to unite people. During his reign, King Harald united many Viking tribes. This unification framed the country of Denmark. His runic symbols are used today on all Bluetooth devices. The founders of Bluetooth chose his runic initials for their company icon.

Another impressive example of a runestone can be found in Sweden. The Rök runestone is a massive structure. It is over eight feet high and weighs over five tons. The runic etchings on the Rök runestone include 28 lines of text that incorporate 760 runes. Deciphering the runes has been a challenge since there are different styles of writing and versions of the Futhark woven through its script.

Varin, a local chieftain, erected the monument to honor his son, Vamoth. The cause of Varin's son's death remains a mystery. The stone includes Norse myths, Viking legends, and family sagas, which all overlap each other. References to historical events are included on the Rök stone. In the 6th century, the sun was obscured for years because of volcanic eruptions. It is not known if this caused Varin to believe that his son's death was inevitable or not. However, inscriptions commissioned by Varin suggest that his son was destined to die. Once Vamoth was dead, he could join the armies of the gods.

Many Vikings believed the runes were magical. The power that came with the ability to write added to the mystical aura of communicating through runes. Runes were believed to provide protection from illnesses, in battles, and against sorceresses. Many thought that the messages inscribed using the runic alphabet contained layers of meaning. Secrets and mysteries were thought to be hidden within the letters and glyphs.

Chapter 8: Art, Design, and Architecture

Viking art and design wove together utilitarian purposes and images that spoke to a deeper meaning. Similar to the use of runes, which were letters and symbols for sounds, to communicate daily ideas, design elements intertwined layers of meaning like the runes' power beyond the literal use of the Futhark. From the Old Norse word for secrets, runes imparted supernatural forces into warriors' shields, amulets, and talismans.

The runic alphabet is closely associated with the god Odin. It was believed that Odin gave this sacred communication to the world. Therefore, the staves and twig impressions were part of the message of and connection to the other world. Casting runes on sticks in a particular manner was a way to understand the world, assist with troubles, and help solve problems. Skilled readers could untangle the message and help people find the symbolic meaning sent in the rune cast.

Runes were not the only means used during the Viking Age to communicate multiple layers of meaning. Visual images intertwined the belief system of the Scandinavian peoples with their cultural icons. Symbols represented the themes and morals that were shared orally through poetry, narratives, and songs. Many Vikings believed in the impact of putting symbols on talismans and artifacts. These mementos with powerful symbols provided the holder reassurance that they could successfully face upcoming challenges.

Vikings used many powerful concrete images to represent intangible concepts. Animals, crosses, depictions of nature, and talismans of the gods frequently appeared in Viking designs. Each of these provided protection and support on one's journey in this world and the next. Evoking assistance from the mystical realm was an important part of the use of amulets.

Decorative patterns combined a mix of emblematic and pragmatic designs. Depictions included on objects and in Viking art revealed beliefs about their gods and goddesses, societal structure, and warrior culture. Viking art is typically examined as six different stylistic periods. The dates and elements of each era overlap each other. Usually, the name of each grouping of art styles is based on the location where the most famous example was found.

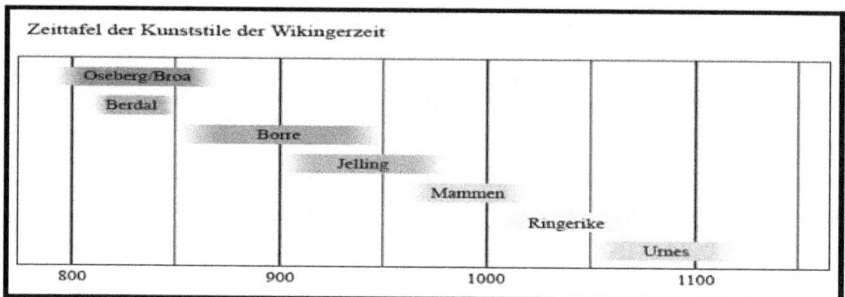

Timeline of Viking art.
Stefan Bollmann, CC BY-SA 3.0 <http://creativecommons.org/licenses/by-sa/3.0/>, via Wikimedia Commons; https://commons.wikimedia.org/wiki/File:Kunststile_der_Wikingerzeit.jpg

The first category of Viking art dates from about 750 to 850 and is referred to as Oseberg/Broa. A Viking burial ship was found at the Oseberg farm in Norway, while a twenty-two-carat gold-leaved horse bridle was discovered at Broa in Gotland, Sweden.

Animals were often depicted in the decorations throughout all six periods of Viking art. Animals etched during the Oseberg/Broa period were abstract and shown in a deconstructed manner. Animals had elongated, looping limbs, oversized protruding eyes, and undersized heads. They are known as ribbon-animals. A mixture of thick and thin lines and knots blended in with the animal shapes.

Art from the Broa area.

*Elisabet Pettersson, Historiska museet/SHM, CC BY 4.0
<https://creativecommons.org/licenses/by/4.0>, via Wikimedia Commons;
https://commons.wikimedia.org/wiki/File:Stora_och_Lilla_Ihre_Grave_174_Pommel_(31020_3).png*

Variations of the animal shapes were noted in the Oseberg area. Illustrations more clearly show the animal's claws grasping one edge of the carving. Within the animal's talons were decorative designs that enhanced the motif. The details are more noticeable due to the variants in surface area.

The Borre period dated from 850 to about 950. Significant artifacts from a burial ship and cemetery were unearthed in Borre, Norway, that contained designs that frame this style of art. Gripping animals continued from the Oseberg style; however, the heads were transformed into triangular shapes.

Artifacts show an increase in geometric designs. Tighter weaves of intricate and interlaced almost-symmetrical lines showcase the animal motif. The ring-chain or ribbon weave designs were created by a continuous looping of the braids and spirals. Some of the swirls and twists are distortions of the animal's body.

Overlapping the Borre style was the Jelling style, which emerged toward the end of the 9th century and concluded before the close of the 10th century. As with the other Viking art styles, Jelling denotes where the items were found. A silver cup with elements of the Jelling style was discovered in burial grounds in Jelling, Denmark.

The characteristics of animals are more ribbon-shaped and less tightly formed than the Borre style. More fluidity was assigned to the S-shaped beasts. Varying geometric lines and images were used to denote the body parts of the animals. More similar to the Broa artifacts, the bodies and heads of the beasts were drawn showing their profile; however, the lines of the illustrations were cleaner, which made the background more prominent. The Jelling style was different from earlier periods of Viking art because of the tendrils or lappets that emanated from the neck of the beast.

Discoveries in a grave site in Mammen, Denmark, provide the naming of the next chronological style of Viking art. An ax head found in the grave is the archetypical representation of this time period, with imagery weaving together Christianity and paganism. The years 950 to 1000 overlap the reign of King Harald Bluetooth and the infusion of Christianity into the lives of the Vikings. Inscriptions on the Jelling runestone, which were commissioned by King Harald, included the Great Beast. King Harald Bluetooth's powerful accomplishments, bringing Christianity to Denmark and controlling Norway, are shown in the motif of the Great Breast.

The Great Beast is a fusion of many animals and emanates strength. It is depicted as a four-legged creature with claw-like feet. Coiled and expanding serpents are woven around the Great Beast. Designs similar to garlands and plants spiral with the snake, creating a sense of robust movement.

Depictions of the Great Beast continued into the Ringerike era, which closed out the 10th century and greeted the 11th century. Commemorative burial stones discovered in Ringerike, Norway, provide the name and style of this grouping of art. Energetic poses of forceful animals were the basis for the stylistic elements. However, Ringerike illustrations were more streamlined and less hectic than Mammen etchings.

Animals continued to be shown in their profile with more complexity than in previous etchings. Thinner whorls of plant-like tendrils coil around beasts. The movement created with the symmetrical strands or antlers emerging from an animal's head gives it a graceful flow.

The culminating period of Viking art is the Urnes style. Relief carvings found on a stave church in Urnes, Norway, exemplified this period's characteristics. This last period is also referred to as the runestone style since depictions were often found on memorial stones throughout the region.

Picture of carvings in Urnes.
Eduardo, CC BY-SA 2.0 <https://creativecommons.org/licenses/by-sa/2.0>, via Wikimedia Commons; https://commons.wikimedia.org/wiki/File:La_pared_original_de_la_Urnes_stavkyrkje_(I).jpg

Sophisticated imprints of the Great Beast were sketched during the Urnes period. Flowing asymmetrical lines formed the animals. The serpent-like creatures were thinner than previously seen and drawn in figure-eight configurations. Elongated features generate a majestic posture in the greyhound-like animal.

Throughout all the art eras of the Viking Age, craftsmen and artisans used art as a means to add decorative elements to everyday objects. The materials chosen to craft the objects were durable and readily available. A vast array of functional objects was transformed through intricate animal designs and abstract lines. Items ranging from shields, weapons, parts of ships, runestones, drinking vessels, jewelry, and more were etched with illustrations.

Relief carvings and engravings were the most common techniques employed by Viking craftsmen. Juxtaposing different materials and colors was another method to create ornate decorations. Some evidence of the use of vivid paints remains, but most of the paint has disintegrated.

In addition to using materials that were easy to find, Vikings also enjoyed working with and wearing adornments made from different metals. Men and women during the Viking Age wore jewelry constructed from gold, silver, and bronze. To obtain these precious metals, Viking merchants and warriors traded for or pillaged these resources. Jewelry was fabricated from locally sourced wood, beads, amber, and glass. Often, the same geometric and animal designs that were used to decorate useable goods were etched on jewelry.

Some jewelry was worn to indicate wealth and status. Other pieces were functional and held together clothing, such as brooches. Valuable adornments served two purposes. Decorative silver jewelry could be used as a means to purchase goods. The value of the silver's weight permitted the wearer to exchange the jewelry to buy other items.

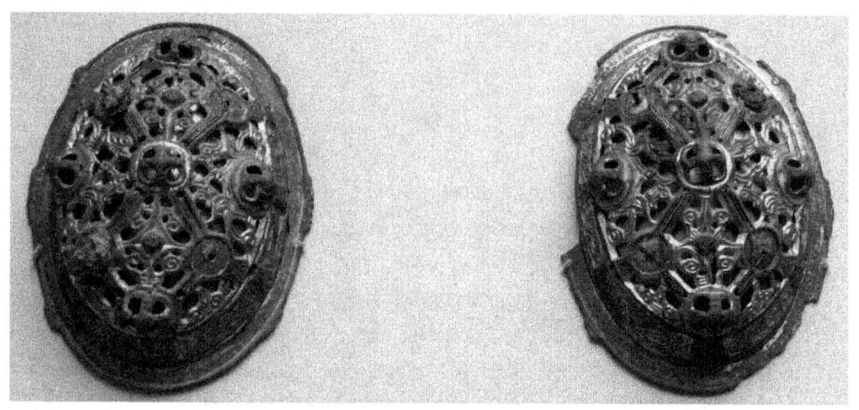

Brooches worn by women.
Johnbod, CC BY-SA 3.0 <https://creativecommons.org/licenses/by-sa/3.0>, via Wikimedia Commons; https://commons.wikimedia.org/wiki/File:Brit_Mus_17sept_015-crop.jpg

Other evidence of the Vikings combining functionality and design is in how they structured and built their villages, hamlets, and towns. One style of building that conveys Viking ingenuity and craftsmanship is the longhouse. The design of the longhouses was similar to the ships in which the Viking warriors sailed. Viking longhouses were constructed with curved walls, which made them appear like inverted ships.

On average, longhouses were between fifteen and twenty-five feet wide. However, longhouses could vary dramatically in length. Most ranged from fifty to sixty-five feet long. Longhouses constructed for the local chieftain or jarl could have extended to 250 feet. Regardless of the longhouse's size, the construction elements were consistent.

Although erected from locally available materials, most longhouses were framed with oak timbers. Areas that did not have readily accessible wood built their homes from stone or peat, creating a different style of house. Two rows of wooden posts were installed throughout the entire length of the home. These wooden timbers bore the weight of the roof.

House roofs were either wood shingles or thatched; sometimes, the roofs were made from vegetation and had moss and grass growing on them. Viking roofs were effective and kept the occupants warm and dry during the cold Scandinavian winters. A hole was shaped in some roofs over the inside fire pit to release smoke.

Walls were often constructed using a method called wooden wattle or wattle and daub. To connect the gaps between the wooden frame, thin strips of wood or sticks woven together (known as wattle) were lashed together between each post. Mud, peat, clay, or animal manure (known as daub) was added to this base layer. The daub created a tacky layer that dried and hardened to form a protective cover.

Inside the longhouse was one large open space. Roof support columns provided a means of separating the area lengthwise into threes. Packed dirt served as the floor. The ashes from the fire pit(s) in the house were added to the earthen floor. The embers helped absorb the moisture and smells. Fires were used for cooking and heating. Some longhouses had multiple fire pits, while others had one centrally located fire; it really depended upon the length of the longhouse.

Benches were embedded in the walls and stretched the length of the longhouse. These wooden benches served multiple functions. They provided extra reinforcement for the walls. The benches also supplied a place for the residents and visitors to eat, work, sit, and sleep. The space under the benches was used for storage. Often, the houses lacked the space for any other furniture. Tables used for eating were collapsible and stored in the rafters when not in use.

Since most Vikings did not have stables for their animals, they were kept at one end of the longhouse. Tools were also stored with the animals. Opposite the barn area of the longhouse was the workspace.

Weaving, sewing, and other household work were performed there. Equipment needed to produce materials, such as a loom, would be located in this section of the longhouse.

Vikings often lived as multigenerational families, so dozens of people might have lived together under one roof. Almost all activities occurred within these crowded homes. The people worked, played, slept, ate, and cooked within the home, especially in the winter. During other seasons, the farm animals would graze outside. The fields would need to be tended, and the animals would need to be cared for.

The open fire was the central gathering area within the longhouse. In addition to providing warmth and a means to cook, fires provided most of the light. Candles were too expensive for most Viking families to afford. After meals, families shared stories and myths of the Viking gods and played games by the light of the fire. However, without chimneys, homes were frequently filled with smoke. The roof vent did alleviate some of the smokiness, but Viking homes were not always healthy places to live.

The longhouses of local leaders were grander than a typical family home. Lavish feasts and banquets were held in the larger and finer longhouses since they had the space and amenities to host impressive social gatherings. These longhouses were the equivalent of medieval castles.

PART THREE: Warfare and Weaponry

Chapter 9: Key Viking Battles

The Vikings made their first appearances on the world stage as talented raiders and warriors with their 793 attack on Lindisfarne Monastery. Their swift and often ruthless strikes led to centuries of assaults along the European coastline, Britain, and Ireland. During these years, the Vikings gained control of the coasts and accessed inland regions, where they established settlements. Numerous clashes occurred as the Scandinavian leaders and kings battled European kings and leaders for dominance.

During the early years of the Viking Age, leaders of raids did not coordinate with others. Raids were often executed with the goal of securing payment to leave the country. However, this changed in 865. The Great Heathen Army arrived in England. Under the coordinated leadership of Ragnar Lothbrok's sons, this army sought to conquer as much of England as they could. Additionally, they sought to seize as many riches as possible from the monasteries.

Though the Kingdom of Northumbria had a larger contingent of soldiers, the battle-tested Vikings were successful. The Great Heathen Army captured the Kingdom of Northumbria and its capital, York. By forming the Kingdom of Jorvik, the Vikings created their first permanent settlement in Britain. The Vikings maintained control of Jorvik until 954. From this location, the Vikings conquered the kingdoms of East Anglia and Mercia.

Only the Kingdom of Wessex was immune to the Vikings' power, part of which was due to the Danegeld paid by King Alfred. This payment ensured the Vikings would leave the Kingdom of Wessex unscathed.

By 878, the Great Heathen Army and its leader, Guthrum, occupied the northern and eastern sections of the Anglo-Saxon world. With this control, Guthrum forced the king of the Anglo-Saxons, Alfred, into exile.

Tired of continually losing land to the Vikings, one of King Alfred's local leaders, Odda, the ealdorman (a high-ranking noble) of Devin, gathered an army to battle the Vikings. Odda led his troops in the Battle of Cynwit, named after the hill on which the battle was fought. The Viking leader in Devan, Ubba, and his warriors surrounded the West Saxon troops. The Anglo-Saxons knew they would perish in their fortress without food or water or die in battle.

The Anglo-Saxons roared out of the fortress with such savage intensity that they surprised the Vikings. Odda and his soldiers killed hundreds of Viking warriors and Ubba, their leader. The win was a moral victory for the Anglo-Saxons. However, their king was still hiding from Guthrum.

Guthrum pursued Alfred, entering the eastern and southern access points of the Kingdom of Wessex. This surprise winter attack forced Alfred and his court to escape to Athelney. While in hiding in the marshes, Alfred and his supporters built a fort. From here, Alfred recruited more troops. He had reassembled his army by the time spring arrived.

After calling a formation at Egbert's Stone, Alfred and his troops marched to Edington. This location was chosen because its boundary was the Viking stronghold of Chippenham. The Anglo-Saxons formed an effective and solid shield wall. The Vikings were hounded back into the fortress and were now the ones faced with starvation. For two weeks, Guthrum and his troops lived under siege. On the fourteenth day, the Vikings surrendered.

Under the treaty Alfred and Guthrum made (the Treaty of Wedmore), the Vikings were forced to withdraw from Wessex. Men and women from Denmark could only live in lands they already controlled in England. Alfred remained king of Kent, Wessex, and West Mercia. The Vikings continued to rule the northern and eastern regions of England, which became known as the Danelaw. People living in the areas stipulated as the Danelaw followed Viking laws and customs. The control of England was now legally divided between the Vikings and the English.

Alfred the Great fully understood the power and fury of the Viking forces. In addition to the provisions in the treaty, Alfred altered his military tactics. He shored up his defenses and began installing border fortresses. The settlement and the growth of burhs, which were fortified towns, were actively advanced. This provided another layer of protection against any future Viking attacks.

The blending of Viking and Anglo-Saxon cultures occurred as part of the Treaty of Wedmore. Another provision of the treaty was that Guthrum and his leaders converted to Christianity. Once Guthrum was baptized, he became Æthelstan. Guthrum also began minting coins following the Anglo-Saxon methods. This stimulated an increase in trade between the Danelaw areas and Anglo-Saxons.

Not all was harmonious between the two groups, especially after the death of Alfred the Great in 899, who strove to unify England. Two claimants declared their right to the throne. One was Alfred's son, Edward the Elder; the other petitioner was his nephew, Æthelwold. When Æthelwold's father and Alfred's older brother, King Æthelred I, died, it was decided that Æthelwold was too young to assume the throne. So, Alfred was declared king instead.

Now that Alfred was dead, Æthelwold wanted what he viewed as his birthright. The Battle of the Holme ensued as a fight for the throne. Æthelwold allied with the Vikings. He was accepted as a leader by the Vikings and led the assault against the Anglo-Saxons in Mercia and northern Wessex. In response, Edward attacked the Vikings in East Anglia, causing the Norsemen to flee to their own lands.

Considering the battle over, Edward withdrew. However, some of Edward's troops remained. The bloody battle continued as Æthelwold and the Viking warriors slaughtered the Anglo-Saxons. However, Æthelwold was killed in the Battle of the Holme, ending his fight for the crown.

Edward's son, Æthelstan, who became king in 924, and his brother, Edmund, led the first unified English forces in their next major battle. The brothers combined their troops from Mercia and Wessex against the invaders. Combined forces from the kingdoms of Dublin, Scotland, and Strathclyde attacked the Anglo-Saxons.

At this time, the land that is now Great Britain was configured differently. Earls of Northumberland, who were of Viking descent, ruled the northern section of today's England. Ireland was led by the Scandinavian Olaf or Anlaf Guthfrithsson, who was king of Dublin. Farther north, in today's Scotland, was the Kingdom of Alba, which was ruled by Constantine II, King of the Scots. The last part of the coalition was from Strathclyde, which was led by Owen I. Strathclyde was on the land that is part of Scotland and Wales.

Another battle between the Vikings and the Anglo-Saxons raged at the Battle of Brunanburh in 937. One of the deadliest battles ever fought on British lands, this was referred to as the Great Battle for years after it occurred. Brunanburh was a pivotal victory in the ongoing hostility between the Scandinavian forces and the Anglo-Saxons. The effects from the battle had lasting effects, some of which are still felt today.

Before the Battle of Brunanburh, Anglo-Saxon territories were ruled by many. Earls continually sought power, land, and leadership roles, resulting in a lack of unification against the invading Vikings. After this battle, the Anglo-Saxon kingdoms transitioned into becoming a unified kingdom. They began working to better secure their borders to the north and west. Eventually, the countries of Scotland, Ireland, and Wales were formed outside of England's boundaries.

While the Great Heathen Army engaged in some battles and other bands of Vikings combated the Anglo-Saxons and others, parties of Vikings continued raining and pillaging. Fear and dread gripped many vulnerable towns and villages along the coast. Many leaders believed the best response to the Viking incursions was to pay the invaders to leave. Others thought they should protect their land and people.

One such leader was the ealdorman of Essex, Byrhtnoth. In 991, as many as three thousand Vikings disembarked on Northey Island off the coast of Essex. Separated from the mainland by the Blackwater Estuary, King Olaf Tyrggvasson and his men waited for the river to recede with the tide.

Tyrggvasson and the Vikings shouted for payments of gold and silver, saying they would leave if their demands were met. Though Byrhtnoth had fewer warriors, he rejected their demands. So, the Battle of Maldon commenced.

As the tide ebbed, the Vikings began their assault. Byrhtnoth's men trapped the Vikings on a narrow strip of land, so the Vikings retreated. After being trapped back on the island, the Vikings asked to be permitted safe crossing so the battle could be fairly fought on one side of the waterway. Very nobly, Byrhtnoth acquiesced and surrendered his advantageous position.

Once the Vikings encountered Byrhtnoth's troops, ferocious fighting ensued. The battle resulted in Byrhtnoth's beheading and a convincing victory for the Vikings. After the battle, King Æthelred paid the Vikings in silver. Some researchers estimate that the Vikings left with up to five tons of silver, worth more than three million dollars today. In addition to soundly defeating Byrhtnoth's men, the Vikings' ability to extract ransom, referred to as Danegeld, made raiding an extremely profitable business.

Relentless Viking raids and demands for Danegeld proved debilitating for King Æthelred. His ability to retain his power and reign were diminishing. In response, Æthelred set up his marriage to Emma, who was of Norman and Viking descent. The king thought Emma would be able to unite the Danes and the Anglo-Saxons.

Æthelred's next political maneuver to address his waning power and belief that the Vikings were plotting his death was to order the deaths of the Scandinavian people living in England. Towns bordering Saxon and Danelaw territories were targeted. Æthelred's directive was enacted on November 13th, 1002, which was St. Brice's Day. The event is now referred to as the St. Brice's Day massacre. Though it was supposedly ordered to be a round-up of men, women, and children, archaeological evidence supports that mainly experienced Viking warriors were targeted.

The total death count is unknown; however, it has been established that the king of Denmark's sister and her husband were killed in the carnage. Sweyn Forkbeard's sister, Gunnhild, and the ealdorman of Devonshire, Pallig Tokesen, her husband, died that day.

Sweyn was known for his brutality, which included the violent toppling of his father's reign (his father was King Harald Bluetooth). For decades, Sweyn had continually raided England, creating a climate of terror. Now that King Æthelred had murdered his sister, Sweyn bombarded England with persistent attacks as retaliation. His attacks were so merciless and relentless that the people of England conceded and named Sweyn their king in 1013. King Æthelred, Emma, and their sons were forced to escape and live in exile.

Sweyn's five-week reign as the first Viking king of Anglo-Saxon lands ended with his death in February 1014. Æthelred and his family returned from exile and coerced Sweyn's son, Cnut, to leave the country.

Cnut began his quest to regain the English throne in 1015. A series of battles with Æthelred's son, Edmund Ironside, for the crown of England climaxed in the Battle of Assandun in October 1016. In the previous four encounters between Cnut and his warriors and Edmund and his troops, Edmund was the victor of three of the battles. Sherston was considered a draw.

Going into Assandun, the numbers of Cnut's forces had been greatly diminished. However, many historians believe a traitor from Edmund's ranks, Eadric Streona, influenced the results at Assandun. Cnut did not trust Eadric, and a year later, Cnut had him killed.

Edmund was not willing to concede the crown and throne but was forced to flee. One last battle stood between Cnut and the power over England. The Battle of Dane's Wood finalized the results of the two-year contest for the throne of England. Cnut soundly defeated Edmund.

In their agreement to cease fighting, King Edmund and Cnut agreed to divide England between themselves. Edmund retained control over Wessex, and Cnut gained the rest of the Anglo-Saxon lands. Also detailed in the treaty was the longevity of the deal. The pact would be enforced until one of the two men died. The surviving man would assume control over the deceased's territory.

Just a couple of months after they made peace, Edmund died. Cnut was now the leader of England. His coronation was held in December 1016. Adding to his power grab, Cnut married Edmund's mother, Emma.

Chapter 10: Armor and Weapons

Weapons were an essential tool during the Viking Age. They added to the ferociousness of the Viking warrior. When attacking villages and pillaging for silver and other valuables, Viking fighters were armed with a variety of weapons. Axes were the most common tool in their arsenal. Access to other weaponry was often dependent on one's wealth and status in society.

Not only were weapons relied upon when raiding, but all free Viking men also wore weapons. All men, other than thralls, were ready to defend their communities, families, and farms. Thralls or slaves were prohibited from carrying any type of weapon. Since most Scandinavians lived on farms during the Viking Age, women and children had knives for their work; in many gravesites of women, there were axes that had been used on the farm.

In a society that valued an honorable reputation, Scandinavian men believed it was not only their right but also their duty to carry a weapon. At night, weapons were kept by each man's bedside. If an attack occurred at night, men were able to readily defend their community.

Since axes were the most affordable, they were the most common weapon. Men from all tiers of society carried an ax for protection. Swords were the costliest weapon, so only the wealthiest men had access to them. Some Vikings also adorned themselves with helmets, spears, knives, and bows and arrows.

When local chieftains or magnates knew they were going raiding, they would conscript the men in the area. Sometimes, it was through a messenger sent by a king. As mentioned before, this king was different than today's royalty. They did not rule an entire country. These kings might have had more power, land, and money than the local earls, so he was able to form an army. All men, including thralls, were expected to respond.

Within five days of the messenger's proclamation, all men met at their leader's ship. Freemen were expected to arrive with weapons, but all were required to appear cleaned, fed, and ready for battle. The warriors used their skills and weaponry to amass treasures. After the raid, the riches were divided among the crew based on rank.

Men of all ranks carried their ax with them to the ship and into battle. Axes used in battle grew to differ from the axes used as farm implements and in shipbuilding and construction. From the commencement of the Viking Age until their power waned, axes used by the Scandinavian warriors became more advanced. An owner's wealth determined the style, size, and shape of axes.

Viking axes found in Norway.
https://commons.wikimedia.org/wiki/File:Viking_axes_Norway.svg

Normally, axes were worn by Viking men on their waists. Belts were fashioned to hold the ax in place. Axes designed for battle had long handles and broader blades than their tool counterparts. Initially, battle axes had steel cutting edges that ranged from three to six inches. Eventually, warriors fought with nine to eighteen-inch sharp steel ax heads. With lightweight handles and a well-balanced wide ax head, Vikings had a deadly advantage in battle. Axes provided the warriors with a broad striking range and agile handling.

Weapons were so important to the Vikings that they often named them (just like many do with their cars or boats today). One of the most well-known battle axes belonged to King Magnus. In 1042, Magnus was named king of Denmark. Sweyn Estridsen disputed this claim. The night before the Battle of Lyrskov Heath, King Magnus believed that his father, Olaf Haraldsson, appeared to him in a dream. Using the dream as a sign, Magnus took up arms against Sweyn for control of Denmark.

Leading his warriors in battle, Magnus used Hel, the battle ax left to him by his father, Saint Olaf. Trusting that Olaf and Hel would guide his men to victory, Magnus and his troops decimated Sweyn's forces, killing over 15,000 men. Snorri Sturluson captured the victory and use of the ax in his collection of sagas about early Scandinavian kings. In *Heimskringla* (*Orb of the World*), Sturluson shared numerous stories about Olaf's reign as king, which included his mystical axe, Hel.

Another weapon commonly used by Viking warriors was the spear. Spears were a versatile weapon for the Scandinavians. Since spears were made using less iron than swords, they were more readily available for the lower classes. Spears were made in two styles. The lighter spears were thrown at enemy combatants. Heavier spears were thrust into the enemy in arm-to-arm combat.

Spears held a special significance to the Vikings. Odin, the Norse god of war and ruler of Valhalla, commenced his battles with Gungnir, his spear. In the first battle of the gods, Odin hurled Gungnir over the enemy and shouted, "Odin owns each of you." Other Viking leaders replicated this act at the start of battles. Viking warriors believed that this offered the enemy to Odin. In return, Odin would protect the Vikings and watch over them. Participating in this ritual would ensure victory with the aid of Odin and his spear.

As with spears, there were two styles of knives used by the Vikings. The most commonly found tool in the tactical belt of the warriors was a knife. Smaller versions of these knives were used as tools. Almost everyone in the Viking Age carried a knife, including thralls. Wealthier warriors used the seax, which was a larger and more deadly knife. Seaxes acted more like a machete in combat.

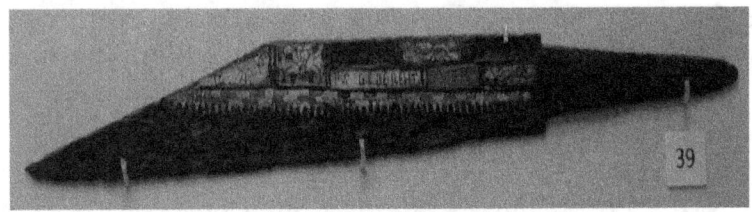

A picture of a seax.
British Museum, CC0, via Wikimedia Commons;
https://commons.wikimedia.org/wiki/File:British_Museum_Sittingbourne_Seax.jpg

Bows and arrows were used for hunting and combat. Bows and arrows balanced out the tools used in hand-to-hand combat. This weapon allowed Vikings to shoot at the enemy when they were farther away. From the bows and arrows recovered from the time period, it is believed the draw force of these Viking weapons reached 90 to 120 pounds of force. This force created a range of between six hundred and seven hundred feet of striking distance.

As part of the Vikings' tactics, Vikings bombarded their adversary with bows and arrows, announcing their arrival. Most Scandinavian warriors could load and reload their bows at rapid speed, shooting twelve arrows a minute. Once the Vikings disembarked from the ships, close-quarter combat began. At this stage of fighting, Vikings relied on other weapons in their arsenal.

The most highly valued weapon of the raiders was the sword. Since swords required the most iron to make of all the weapons, they were the most expensive to produce. Therefore, only the elite had access to swords, which made them a symbol of status and distinction in the Viking Age. Owning swords had such a glorious reputation that they were given as gifts or handed from one generation to the next in the same family.

After participating in a Viking raid or two, the treasures pillaged and distributed among the crew usually enabled a raider to buy a decent sword. Those of higher status were able to have their swords produced with elaborate embellishments. The creation of a sword could take up to one month. In the Icelandic saga about the people of Laxárdalr, the cost of a sword is equal to the value of sixteen dairy cows.

Swords were not carried as part of the Viking utility belt. They had special holders called scabbards. These cases were made from leather or wood. Scabbards were strapped across the warrior's right shoulder. While this made the swords readily available, they were not often used in battle. Instead, many warriors wore their swords to show their rank.

Swords smithed for the initial Viking raids bent easily in battle because they were produced from poor-quality iron. When the process of pattern welding began to be used by Viking blacksmiths, the quality of swords improved.

By using pattern welding, a more durable blade was crafted. Blacksmiths pieced together sections of iron with varying compositions. They were then coiled together and shaped under extreme heat. A talented blacksmith could distribute the iron of varying levels of carbon to generate an equilibrium of maneuverability and hardness in the metal. Then they shaped the sword from the molten mixes of iron.

An even higher quality sword appeared in the armaments of Vikings in the early 9th century. Just over 170 of these swords have been found by archaeologists. Evidence shows that the production of the Ulfberht swords ended around the year 1000.

How the steel was forged for these swords remains uncertain. There are credible theories that explain how the steel was produced. There is evidence of crucible steel, which is what the Ulfberht swords were fashioned from, being used in the area of modern-day India around 300 BCE. The steel appears again in the Viking era and then not again until the 1740s.

Scholars believe the Vikings encountered this material in their travels, either to the Frankish kingdoms nearby or from central Asia. Many researchers believe the Vikings learned the technology needed to produce this superior metal and weapon. They also gathered necessary materials on their voyages, which was why production ceased around 1000. This timing coincides with Russia interfering with the Viking trade routes.

Regardless of how the Vikings acquired this technology and necessary materials, manufacturing crucible steel was an incredible feat. Producing steel for Ulfberht swords necessitated the involvement of many blacksmiths. Master craftsmen and their apprentices worked diligently to accomplish this task, from the fabrication of the steel to the shaping of the blade to the formation of the handles to the creation of jeweled embellishments.

These swords provided the Vikings with a superior advantage in battle. Ulfberht swords were lighter than swords made from the iron used for other weapons. Warriors could effortlessly manipulate their swords in battle. Since high-carbon steel is somewhat flexible, the swords did not break or snap as readily. Crucible iron creates a strong material, so the blades of these swords retained their sharpness throughout the fight.

The iron was liquified to eliminate impurities. No evidence exists of furnaces that could reach the level of heat required for the process, so it is thought the Viking blacksmiths hammered the impurities from the iron ore. Then carbon was added to the molten iron to strengthen it. Analysis of Ulfberht swords revealed they are comprised of almost three times the carbon of other iron used during this era.

Swords made from this steel were stamped with the inscription of Ulfberht (two crosses and a T). Initially, some researchers thought this was a blacksmith's trademark. However, since the swords were crafted for over three hundred years, it is now thought the inscription was used by those who could create this steel.

The swords fashioned from crucible iron were so amazing that forgeries were made. Swords that have been discovered have the requisite two crosses and Ulfberht without the T. Warriors who had the good fortune to use these swords and others who watched with amazement at what they accomplished believed there were supernatural elements at work in the creation of the swords.

Only blacksmiths and their workers understood the craft. This added to the mysteriousness associated with the power of Ulfberht swords and metalworking in general. In the early years of the Viking Age, most blacksmiths worked with all metals. As time progressed, blacksmiths became more specialized and worked with iron and steel. Craftsmen shared their knowledge of the trade with their apprentices, who were often family members. Shrouding their skills in mystery added to the supernatural aura connected with the swords.

Villages that had their own blacksmiths were fortunate. Smiths crafted weapons for warriors and homeowners, produced items for the home, and fashioned tools for the farm. Having someone with this level of skill added to the self-sufficiency of a community. Kings and high-ranking jarls had their own blacksmiths.

Myths depict the magical ability of blacksmiths to forge tools and weapons for the gods. The naming of weapons for gods and warriors emphasized the power of these armaments. Kennings (elaborate descriptive phrases) were often created to enhance the owner's importance and the mystical ability of the sword, ax, or spear.

Sometimes, a combination of two or three words to create a phrase, such as leg-biter, foot-biter, or hole-maker, was used for swords. For those fortunate enough to have swords with a lineage, the kenning on the sword talked about the ancestral connections to the weapon. Summoning the name of Wolf's Claws while entering battle infused the warrior with the strength and cunning of a wolf.

Chapter 11: Viking Ships

The Vikings' military tactics and ability to finesse their weapons in battle made them indomitable and feared foes for hundreds of years. However, without their shipbuilding expertise, the Vikings' dominance would not have occurred. When the longship with a snakehead on its prow sailed over the horizon into the view of those on land, the people knew they should be afraid. And that's just what the Vikings wanted.

In addition to raiding, Viking ships allowed the Norse to explore and expand their territories. Vikings discovered trade routes, which enabled them to foster their settlements and establish towns for trading.

The geographical foundations of the homelands of the Scandinavians facilitated their quest for methods to traverse waterways. Rivers, fjords, lakes, straits, and the ocean surrounded and summoned the early Scandinavians. As early as 350 BCE, early canoes were carved from local trees, providing a way to navigate the lands. Between then and the dawn of the Viking Age, Scandinavian water vessels were dramatically transformed.

During the Middle Ages, there were two main methods of shipbuilding. One was the carvel. The frames of the wooden boats and ships made in this manner were constructed first. Planks were then fastened to the frames. The timber used in the assembly was cut with saws. The sawn timber was cut across the grain of the wood, which weakened the strength of the wood beams. Therefore, boats following the carvel build had a harder time sailing the currents of the water, producing a rocky and slow passage.

With their vast timber resources, the Vikings were able to build their watercraft using the clinker style. Unlike the carvel, the outside of a clinker boat was erected first. The frame of the vessel was constructed later in the shipbuilding process. Carvel boats could be built with any quality of timber, but clinker vessels required the superior timber from pine and oak trees. Both trees were readily available for Scandinavian shipbuilding. Unseasoned or green wood was used in the formation of clinker vessels since it is pliable.

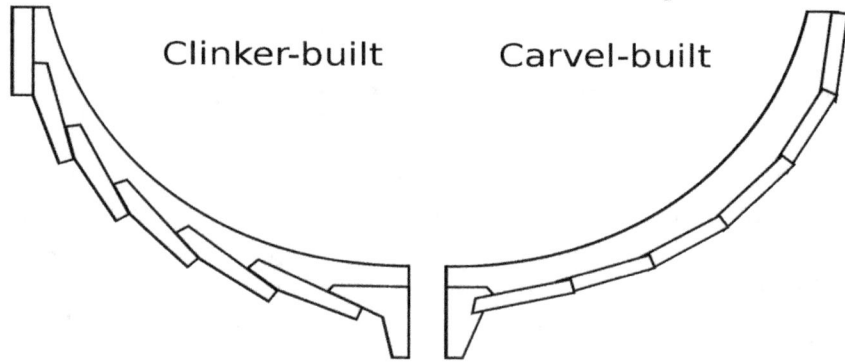

Diagram of clinker and carvel shipbuilding.
https://commons.wikimedia.org/wiki/File:Clinker-carvel.svg

Oak timbers were used for the keel, which extended the length of the ship and created the centerline. Viking shipbuilders were some of the first to frame boats with keels, which added stability to the vessel. The stern and stem were then attached to the keel. Overlying planks were attached with rivets to add durability to the hull. Animal hair and spruce roots were threaded together to tie the planks to the frame of the ship.

The additional strength from this part of the clinker method created a lighter frame. Viking ships were also more flexible, allowing them to bend and roll with the waves. Joints were filled with scrap materials and covered with tar to make them watertight. The construction of the hulls allowed the ships to sail in shallow watercourses; the heavier carvel boats were not functional for them.

Viking shipbuilders were adept at using their axes. Instead of the harshness of sawing timbers, Scandinavian craftsmen were able to create subtle incisions in the wood. By carving with the grain of the wood, Vikings created stronger, more flexible, and lighter ships. Viking warriors were able to sail in many different waterways.

Since the Vikings traveled on many different-sized waterways for a variety of purposes, many styles of boats were crafted. Most water vessels used by the Scandinavians were functional and necessary for daily chores and life. Fishing, visiting other villages, and transporting goods and people created the need for small boats for many. These sailed up and down rivers, back and forth across lakes, and short distances along the coastline.

For trading purposes, the Vikings required vessels that could withstand the power and unpredictability of the oceans. Viking trade routes were extensive. The boats that carried traders and their goods were essential to the Scandinavians' expansion of wealth and power. Longboats, which were synonymous with the Viking raiders, were not appropriate for the work of traders.

Sturdiness and reliability were the two key characteristics of merchant ships. These ships were constructed to carry cargo; therefore, they featured broader and deeper hulls for storage. Arriving at each port intact was more important than the speed of the boat. These attributes were balanced with the weight of the ships. Merchant ships sailed through different waterways, so merchant ships were often conveyed by the crew over shallow, non-passable sections of water or harbors.

To accommodate the numerous waterways that the traders navigated, they built two types of trading ships. Knarrs were designed to carry heavy cargo on long ocean voyages; some knarrs had the capacity to hold over forty tons of freight and passengers. Due to their heavy freight, these merchant ships relied on wind power and were propelled by a large mast. On days with strong winds, knarrs sailed up to seventy-mile miles. Crews averaged about thirty men, so they could maximize their weight capacity with cargo.

Model of a knarr.
Europabild,, CC BY-SA 3.0 <https://creativecommons.org/licenses/by-sa/3.0>, via Wikimedia Commons; https://commons.wikimedia.org/wiki/File:Modell_Knorr.jpg

For inland trading routes, Vikings designed the byrdings to carry lighter cargo. Scandinavian crews whose shipping lanes were more difficult to maneuver sailed in byrdings. The boats were equipped with oars and a large sail, which was similar to the knarrs. However, the crew, consisting of about fifteen men, mainly used oars to manipulate the boat. Merchandise and their merchants were transported rapidly from port to port in byrdings.

Ships designed to carry more warriors than cargo were the iconic Viking longships. Carved with elaborately designed bows, often depictions of frightening animals, longships signified that bloodshed was imminent. Dubbed dragonships by the British, the sight of one of these magnificent vessels spread terror throughout the land.

Early versions of longships were used as early as the 6th century BCE. Viking longships evolved during the Viking Age into four main classifications. However, they all followed a similar design. They were designed to navigate water ranging from rough seas to shallow estuaries. Longships could sail in rivers with water as low as three feet. This permitted the warriors to skim the surface of the water and leap out of the ship and into battle. Other vessels were outfitted with small rowboats that enabled the Vikings to get to shore without damaging the longship.

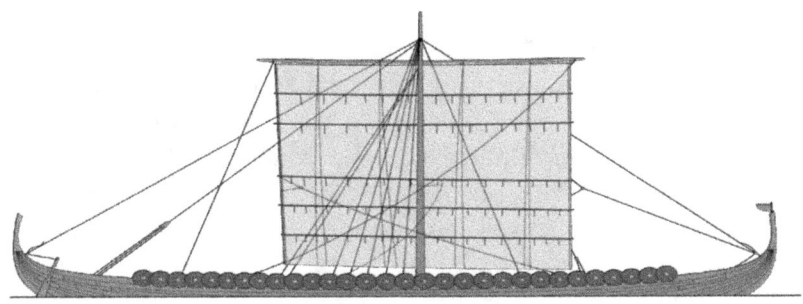

Sketch of a Viking longship.
https://commons.wikimedia.org/wiki/File:Viking_longship.png

Another characteristic of the longships that aided the Vikings in their successful raids was their ability to reverse sail without physically turning the boat around. Longships were designed to be double-ended, so they could sail forward or backward. The longships were equipped with a mast, sail, and oars, so Vikings could manually row their boats if there was no wind to propel the ship.

Piloting longships was accomplished utilizing one oar that was attached to the side of the ship. Referred to as the steerboard, the operator stood on the right stern or rear of the ship. He piloted the boat by moving the oar in the direction they sailed. Over time, the steerboard evolved into starboard or the right side of a boat.

As the scope and frequency of Viking raids grew, their longboats evolved to better meet their needs. Ships with an increased cargo capacity and the ability to carry additional crew members and sail farther distances were designed and built.

Four main classes of longships emerged from the Viking Age. The karvi class of longships was created for smaller raiding forays. Crews averaged about thirty warriors when the boats were used for battle. Due to their more diminutive size, karvi boats could not traverse as far as others on the open ocean waters. They were used in raids, but the versatile boats were often used for other domestic purposes.

The snekkja was the class of ship built and sailed most frequently. It had a crew of about forty men and was equipped with twenty pairs of oars. These ships were easier for shipbuilders to frame since they were only about sixty feet long. Though smaller than the Viking warships, snekkjas could still accommodate the rewards of a fruitful raid.

The success of the Viking raids led to the addition of new types of longships to enable the warriors to capitalize on their triumphs. The next class of Viking longship, the skeid, was bigger and more seaworthy. These intimidating vessels, which could be over one hundred feet long, were constructed to carry seventy warriors. The skeids were powered with sails and had up to thirty pairs of oars.

Viking warships, or the busse class, were the most impressive of all Viking longships. Those sailing aboard a busse ship were able to travel much farther distances across the ocean. Larger cargo areas could store supplies for long distances and the rewards garnered once the raiders landed ashore. These ships were much longer than other longships at 160 feet and could house a crew of 80 warriors. As with other longboats, the busse could be propelled by the thirty-five sets of oars or its sails.

The busse class is also referred to as the drakkar or dragonships because of the ferocious dragon or serpent head carved into the stem on the bow of the ship. The intimidating animal design was often continued to the stern of the ship with the dragon's or serpent's tail. Adding to the terrorizing visual of the ships was the addition of wings created from the sails and legs of the beast from the oars. The dragonships led the fleet and announced the arrival of the pillaging warriors.

Many Viking ships used shield lists or shield racks. These were railings on which the warriors displayed their shields. Viking shields were often decorated or painted with different patterns, scenes of Norse gods, or runic writings. The Viking ship discovered at Gokstad was found with sixty-four yellow and blue shields. The shields added to the mystique of the dragon or serpent head looming on the water. Many researchers also believe that the shields offered protection from the wind and rain. Since this added drag to the ship, other researchers surmise that the shields were not needed for weather protection since they were not hung on the wall until the ship was nearing its destination. Then the shields were mounted as protection from the enemy's arrows and spears. When the warriors disembarked, they grabbed their shields to use in battle.

Initially, powerful chieftains or jarls oversaw the raids. In the later years of the Viking Age, kings and military leaders assumed responsibility for the planning and execution of raids and retaliatory attacks against other leaders. When the Viking raids and conquests grew in complexity, they gathered a combination of all types of longships. Records indicate that the Vikings organized fleets that were comprised of hundreds of ships.

To accomplish these attacks, Viking leaders required extensive knowledge of the opposing armies. Many phases of planning were needed to gather the ships, warriors, and supplies from different villages and towns. It was an amazing strategic and logistical feat for the Vikings to accomplish.

Not only were the Vikings master shipbuilders and logisticians, but they were also highly skilled navigators. On some of their first forays, the Vikings maintained sight of the shoreline, with natural landmarks guiding their course. Their experiences were shared with other Viking navigators. It appears that as they ventured away from the coast, Vikings utilized islands as guideposts.

Their knowledge of nature aided in their ability to chart sea courses. Viking sailors used bird sounds to know when land was nearby. Floki Vilgerdarson used the assistance of ravens when he sailed from Norway in search of present-day Iceland. Vilgerdarson released three ravens. One bird flew back toward the Faroe Islands; another returned to the ship. The third raven soared off ahead of the boat; Vilgerdarson followed the raven's trajectory and sailed to Iceland.

Other elements of the natural world guided the Scandinavian sailors. The color of the water indicated changing temperatures, which provided information about their location on the water and their proximity to different types of watercourses. Directional shifts of the wind also provided seamen with information on the direction they should pilot their boats.

Looking toward the heavens and the location of the moon, sun, and stars provided a wealth of lore and data for early mariners. The least experienced navigator could use the sunrise and sunset to navigate easterly and westerly courses. With more time on the open water, a veteran seafarer could chart their course following the movement of the stars.

Tools were developed to aid the ship's navigator during the daylight hours when stars were not visible. One instrument was the bearing dial or circle. This device provided information about the latitude of the ship. An upright pin was placed in the middle of a platform with a pointer. Shadows created on the platform indicated the position of the sun.

At noon, the ship's navigator used a sun shadow board to verify their course. Sailors placed a board in a bowl of water to keep it level. A pin or gnomon indicated the location of the sun. Circles on the board noted regions to which they should sail in order to stay on course. If the shadow fell outside the circled area, the ship had sailed out of range.

To obtain navigational information on cloudy days, Scandinavian seamen employed the use of a sunstone. Calcite, also called an Icelandic spar, was held up in the light. Depending upon the color of the stone, the Vikings knew the position of the sun and their ship's location.

Sunstone.
ArniEin, CC BY-SA 3.0 <https://creativecommons.org/licenses/by-sa/3.0>, via Wikimedia Commons; https://commons.wikimedia.org/wiki/File:Silfurberg.jpg

To share the knowledge gained through experiences, the Vikings created songs, chants, and rhymes. In these mantras and tunes, directions to different locations were communicated. Routes to avoid because of navigational or other dangers could be conveyed through repetitive refrains. The Scandinavians' shipbuilding expertise, navigational knowledge and tools, and chants for easy recall aided warriors and traders.

Chapter 12: More than Warriors - Viking Traders

Vikings are well renowned for their skills as raiders. To be effective marauders, Vikings needed access to other countries to loot and seize riches and treasures, so they sailed in ships they designed and built. Their incredible ability to construct ships for different waterways and purposes made them successful traders as well. Most men during the Viking Age sailed as traders and not as part of a raiding party. What the Scandinavian people could not produce themselves, they bartered and traded with other villages and people.

Raiding ships constructed by the Vikings were known for their seaworthiness and ability to maneuver rivers and oceans. With the clinker style, Vikings widened the raiding ships to create room for cargo and built the knarr and byrding vessels for trading. Some trading ships spanned more than twenty feet in width and were seventy feet long. With the ability to transport more than sixty tons of payload, the Vikings profited handsomely from their trading routes.

The collapse of the Western Roman Empire provided the Vikings access to more trade routes. Viking trade was integral in redeveloping Europe's economy after the fall of Rome. The location of the Scandinavian lands provided the Viking traders with relatively easy access to a multitude of trade routes. To the west, the Vikings could sail the waters of the North Atlantic Ocean to Britain, Ireland, and Spain. To their east, the Scandinavians traversed the Dnieper and

Volga Rivers to reach the lands of Russia, Constantinople, and much of the Middle East and Asia.

Typically, traders from today's Sweden sailed the eastern trade routes, and Danish merchants and sailors navigated the westward waterways. Whether the traders went east or west, they usually carried cargos of Scandinavian riches of fur, walrus tusks, amber, and iron. Those who sailed the western routes were also known for their raiding and pillaging. However, when the raiders encountered towns that were not suitable for raiding, those locations became part of the western trade route.

In addition to establishing trade routes and trading centers, many Scandinavians also moved their families to these locations. Up and down the coastlines, towns became settled by the Scandinavians. Dublin, Normandy, and York were just a few of the cities that the Vikings helped establish and grow.

In their new locales, transplanted Vikings recreated their workshops so they could continue to produce goods to trade. Tradesmen often created pottery, combs, leather goods, jewelry, and glass beads that had previously been made in Scandinavia. Viking armaments were also crafted in the towns where Vikings resettled. Over time, the Scandinavians and locals intermarried.

When the Vikings sailed east, they were propelled by the same motivations as their forays to the west: raiding and pillaging. However, accessing the lands via river routes limited the Vikings' ability to effectively execute their hit-and-run strikes on poorly defended coastal towns. On their river voyages, the Vikings were vulnerable to surprise attacks. These ambushes and the lack of readily accessible cities or monasteries to pillage made these expeditions costly for raiding parties. To effectively pursue their goal of gaining wealth, the Vikings needed to establish home bases from where they could operate.

As traders, the Vikings were the first to navigate the waters of the Volga and Dnieper Rivers. Profitable trading centers and routes were created along the Dnieper River to the Black Sea. Scandinavian traders sailed the Volga River to access the Caspian Sea. Similar to their western voyages, Vikings helped establish trading towns along these routes.

By the end of the height of their days of trading, the Vikings constructed a trade network that included Europe, Russia, India, the

Middle East, and parts of China. Vikings had traded as far as the Baltic Sea before they expanded their reach as traders and raiders. With the development of their ships, Vikings were now able to traverse the rivers between the Black and Caspian Seas.

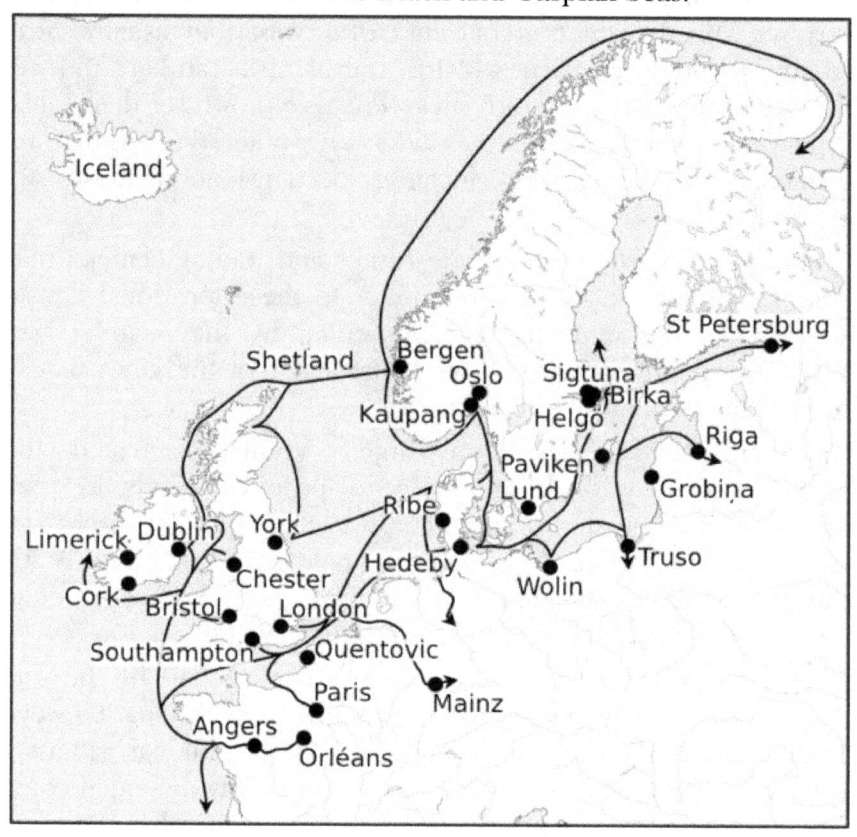

Map of Viking routes.
Brianann MacAmhlaidh, CC BY-SA 4.0 <https://creativecommons.org/licenses/by-sa/4.0>, via Wikimedia Commons; https://commons.wikimedia.org/wiki/File:Viking_Age_trade_routes_in_north-west_Europe.png

Eventually, Scandinavian traders traveled these waterways and connected to the capital of the Byzantine Empire, Constantinople, which is present-day Istanbul, Turkey. Without the interference from the Romans, the Scandinavian traders reached the Silk Road, which provided access to the Far East. Through these routes, Scandinavian traders brought back silver, silk fabrics, exotic spices, wines, and other treasures not available in Scandinavia. Viking traders created a web of trading ports that encompassed the world as they knew it.

The first Scandinavian people who established themselves along these river routes were referred to as the Rus. The Old Norse word *rópsmenn* (meaning route or rowers), which referred to how the Vikings appeared in this region, is believed to be the origin of the Rus. Another term coined by the Greeks to refer to Scandinavians was Varangians. Thought to have originated from the Norse language, Varangian has its roots in the word *vár* for "pledge." The Varangians, while associated with trade, were more often used as the noted bodyguards of the emperor of the Byzantine Empire. "Rus" is more commonly used as the nomenclature for Nordic tradesmen and merchants. However, both terms refer to Scandinavians.

The Varangian or Volga trade route established by the Norse traversed almost two thousand miles of waterways. Beginning in Sweden, the tradesmen on the route sailed over the Baltic Sea to the Gulf of Finland through different rivers and lakes to the Black Sea, ending in Constantinople. In addition to a pathway to access riches and treasures, trade along the Volga and Dnieper Rivers resulted in the growth of cities and towns.

Scandinavian traders who preferred the role of Viking warrior were able to serve as mercenaries for the Byzantine Empire. Emperor Basil II was in dire need of assistance, as he sought to fight off three challengers to his rule. So, Basil turned to the north for support. Vladimir, the ruler of Kievan Rus', which was close to Sweden, had access to Viking warriors. To support Basil II, Vladimir shared six thousand of his transplanted Vikings with the Byzantine emperor. In return, Basil promised his sister to Vladimir in marriage.

This elite fighting force repelled the advances of those seeking to overthrow Basil. Basil II established the Varangian Guard, ensuring that he had his own personal protective unit that he could trust. Basil disbanded his Greek bodyguards in favor of the Viking-based militia band. The role of the Varangian Guard varied, but they were always ready to fulfill any order from the emperor.

These men were mercilessly devoted to the emperor and accompanied Basil everywhere he or his family traveled, including church services. The mercenary force performed underhanded duties when the emperor ordered them to do so, with the guards arresting anyone disloyal to Basil. They also acted as jailers at the infamous prison of Nóumera.

Another unit of these fearsome fighters guarded the city limits. Also included in the Varangians were bands of elite Vikings. This group accompanied the emperor in battle. This unit's ability to fight successfully aided the Byzantines in numerous battles. Since only the best of the best were accepted in the Varangian Guard, it provided the exclusive group with a high status when they returned to their homelands. Being a guard proved to be an extremely lucrative job. The lure of battle and glory associated with victory made this a desirable occupation. Harald Hardrada, who became King Harald III of Norway, fought in the legendary ranks of these Viking warriors.

Scandinavians not only left their mark as warriors, but tradesmen also transformed the landscape with settlements established to foster trade. With their incredible ship-making talents, the Scandinavians were flexible about where they could dock their boats because they did not require intricate harbors. Boats could be carried overland when necessary, even if they were filled with cargo. Oars were slotted through the slots and used to lift the boats. Trade and the resulting trading centers were an outgrowth of the adventures of the Scandinavian seamen.

Many towns arose adjacent to naturally occurring harbors, which varied in size and status. The trading centers were often centrally located and began to connect the scattered farms and fishing areas. Since the goods being brought to trade were valuable, it was important for the developing areas to be protected; otherwise, traders would refuse to return to that location.

Local kings and chieftains facilitated the development of markets into towns. Taxes were levied on goods bought and sold at the market. The leaders utilized the income from taxes to pay for the costs of protecting the town. Markets grew and thrived in locations that were readily defensible and easily accessible by land and the sea. Kings and local leaders were also instrumental in obtaining land if they did not already own it.

Initially, the markets were only open for trading in warmer weather. As they grew, more people moved to the towns. Craftsmen relocated their shops to larger trading centers. Farms surrounded the marketplaces and fed the visiting traders and the people who lived in the village.

Trading centers were so profitable that it is believed that King Gudfred attacked the town of Reric in 808. Reric was located outside of his jurisdiction, but once the Danish king eliminated the competition of Reric, he helped grow Hedeby in present-day Denmark. The tradesmen who previously sold their wares in Reric were forced to relocate to land within Gudfred's domain. To make his trading center more appealing, Gudfred had the Danevirke, a Danish fortification system, rebuilt. This created a more secure boundary around Hedeby.

Another important trading town was Ribe. Located on the shores of the North Sea and the Ribe River, traders from other areas were able to access the marketplace because of Ribe's harbor. New evidence is emerging that Ribe, located in present-day Denmark, was the first Scandinavian town. Archaeologists are finding proof that Ribe was a trading center more than fifty years before the Viking warriors raided the monastery at Lindisfarne. This suggests that expeditions that originated from Scandinavian lands peacefully sailed to import and export goods with others. Ribe grew in size and importance as the Viking raids and trading increased.

The trading center of Staraya Ladoga is also believed to have been established before the attack on Lindisfarne. Situated in present-day western Russia across from Finland, Staraya Ladoga linked the Baltic and Black Seas for seafaring traders. Research indicates that Scandinavian traders first settled this market town in the 750s, again well before the first documented Viking raid in 793. Initially, Scandinavian traders arrived with their goods during the summer months. By the middle of the next century, evidence shows that craftsmen inhabited the town on a year-round basis.

As the number of Scandinavian settlements grew on the eastern trade routes, these Scandinavians became known as the Volga Vikings. Their initial forays into trade were the exchange of furs for silver and other goods from central Asia. Accounts from Arabs Abu'l ibn Khordadbeh and Ahmad ibn Fadlan describe in detail the Volga Vikings, who sailed the Volga River and traded at marketplaces along that route. Trading posts along the Volga eventually led to settlements on the Dnieper River and the Black Sea. Once traders and sailors reached the Black Sea, they gained entry to the Mediterranean Sea and a new world of riches.

Scandinavian traders sought to extend their influence beyond just the goods they sold. They established their own trading centers so they could control the goods that were traded and collect revenue. Slavic lands and areas beyond offered highly profitable items to trade, so the Norsemen began controlling the settlements that arose along their eastern trade routes. This loosely connected string of towns is often referred to as Kievan Rus'. Initial attempts by the Norse to unify the villages were met with resistance.

However, over time, the Norse gradually became the rulers of the waterways and marketplaces, including preferential trading status in Constantinople. The eastern Vikings used different tactics than their contemporaries who sailed west, but it worked out well for them since they dictated the flow of trade and items traded.

In the Vikings' conquests of market towns, raids on monasteries and unprotected villages, and after dominating in battles, the Vikings enslaved those they captured. This opened up another profitable avenue for the Scandinavian traders. The people that the Vikings seized were wanted by buyers at the markets in Constantinople and farther east. The enslaved people sold by the Vikings were from all areas of the known world.

Bartering served as the basis for many trading deals. However, as the Vikings expanded their raiding and trading routes, they had more access to coins, gold, and silver. The Scandinavians created their own dies and minted coins to use in trade. With time, the Vikings became more sophisticated as they developed a market economy. Traders often carried their own scales to ensure they received the exact amount of silver and bronze in exchange for their goods.

Coins for trading.

EttuBruta, CC BY-SA 4.0 <https://creativecommons.org/licenses/by-sa/4.0>, via Wikimedia Commons; https://commons.wikimedia.org/wiki/File:Viking_weight_combined_only_reflection.jpg

PART FOUR: Myth and Mythology

Chapter 13: Customs, Rituals, and Religion

The Scandinavians who lived during the Viking Age did not leave any written texts that researchers can explore today. Much of what is known or theorized about the Scandinavians was shared by other cultures with whom they interacted. Other information was written years after the Viking Age. Many who wrote about them and their culture viewed the Vikings and their beliefs through the lens of time and other religions.

Customs, rituals, and religious practices and beliefs of the Vikings did not occur weekly at a church service. Ceremonies celebrating or commemorating life, death, or marriage were shared communally. Other beliefs differed from region to region and among people within a geographical area. Similar gods and goddesses were worshiped, but there was not a definite observance that one had to follow. Believers were free to worship deities who were relevant to their own personal life and experiences. Therefore, there were a number of ways to pay homage to one's gods and ancestors.

The local chieftain or ruler of an area often led a community's religious and ritualistic celebrations. However, they may have relied upon traveling or local seeresses. These women, also referred to as völur or *völva*, possessed mystical and magical abilities. Pre-Christian Scandinavian seeresses were proficient in their practice of magic, which was referred to as *seidr*. Seeresses would enter a trance-like state, which enabled the practitioner to enter the world of spirits. She then transported herself between this realm and the next to collect information that aided her prophecies.

Engraving of two völvas.
https://commons.wikimedia.org/wiki/File:Ed0048.jpg

The Scandinavian people believed that the seeresses could view their fate and manipulate events to influence their outcomes. With this knowledge, she could foretell their futures and work with the villagers on constructing new experiences to live within their fated world. Local leaders were assisted in ritualistic events by the seeress. Performing ceremonial rites and traditions could lead to better weather and harvests or successes in battles.

Ceremonies surrounding key life events were performed in Scandinavian communities. Births were an exciting yet dangerous event. Therefore, preparation for birth began while the mother was pregnant. Community and family members sang ritual songs that were intended to protect the mother and unborn child with their invocations to the goddesses Frigg and Freya.

After a child's birth, the baby had to be accepted into the family. First, the baby had to nurse on their mother's breast. Nine nights later, the father's ritual to acknowledge his baby was performed. The father placed the newborn on his knee, and then the infant was sprinkled with water. Lastly, the father named the child. Usually, ancestral names were selected or those of locally worshipped deities.

After these steps, the child was now a member of the family. With familial acceptance, the child had all the same rights as other clan members, such as inheritance. Children who were not accepted by their parents could be placed outside in the elements and left to die. Those born with abnormalities or to families who could not care for a baby could choose to let their baby die due to exposure. However, once an infant was accepted, the parents could not put the baby to death; if they did, they would be accused of murder.

Another significant occurrence in the Scandinavian world was marriage and its customs. Boys became men once they lived through fifteen winters; girls were of a marrying age as soon as they turned twelve. Before courting began, thought was given to whether or not the courtship would result in marriage. Otherwise, the woman's family would be humiliated if the wooing did not end with a proposal for her. If a proposal were turned down by the woman, the man's family would feel demeaned. These hurt feelings could result in violent retribution.

Once a successful courtship bloomed, the suitor and his family would go to the woman's house. A proposal for marriage would be made to the woman's caretaker; it is not known if she always had input on the decision. In essence, a contract had to be agreed upon for the marriage to proceed. As part of the betrothal, a *mundr* or bride-price was paid to the bride's family by the groom's clan. The bride's father offered a *heimangerð* or dowry, which would be brought to the wedding. The fathers of the bride and groom shook hands in front of witnesses to finalize the agreement, which included the date of the marriage ceremony.

Usually, the wedding would occur within one year from the handshake. Marriages were on Fridays (Freya's day) to ensure that the goddess of marriage bestowed her blessings of love and fertility. Frequently, the couple and their guests celebrated for three or more days with elaborate feasts at the bride's parents' house. The couples professed vows of fidelity to each other. Once witnesses saw the couple in their bed, the marriage contract was considered consummated.

At the same marriage bed, divorce proceedings could be initiated. Observers were summoned by the woman to her home. While standing next to her and her husband's bed, the wife could state her desire for a divorce. Sometimes, the marriage contract stipulated the terms of a divorce. Financial entanglements that ensued from a divorce could result in long-lasting battles between the families. However, divorces because the couple did not have children could be dissolved without complications.

Evidence from graves provides clues about ceremonies and rituals surrounding death during the Viking era. Most Scandinavian people were either cremated or buried. Very few were actually buried in Viking ships; those ceremonies were reserved for high-ranking kings, queens, or chieftains. Researchers have not discovered any evidence of ships being set ablaze and pushed out to sea. The dramatic scenes of fiery boats taking the deceased to their next life are only found in myths or the epic poem *Beowulf*.

Graves from the Viking Age that have been located show that most people were buried with goods. These artifacts varied depending upon a person's status while they were alive, but the grave goods included jewelry, weapons, and tools to assist the dead in their next life. It is believed that those who chose to be cremated were burned with their grave goods. The smoke from the burial pyre was thought to assist the deceased in their journey to the afterworld.

A Viking burial site.
Mpravink1993, CC BY-SA 4.0 <https://creativecommons.org/licenses/by-sa/4.0>, via Wikimedia Commons; https://commons.wikimedia.org/wiki/File:Lindholm_H%C3%B8je_Dec08.jpg

Framing their belief in an afterlife was the perception of one's soul. Many Vikings believed that each person's body was composed of four elements. All four parts complemented each other; none was more valuable or essential than any other part of the soul.

Physical looks were referred to as *hamr*. One's *hamr* was expected to transform throughout their life. A person's mind could influence their physical appearance or *hamr*. The belief in berserkers or warriors whose appearance became altered was due to the mind or *hugr* altering the body. Even after death, a person's *hamr* remained in this world.

Following the soul into the afterlife was the *hugr*. A person's identity or disposition was captured in one's *hugr*. A Scandinavian person's mindfulness and approach to life was part of their *hugr*. The Scandinavians believed that infants inherited their ancestor's character traits.

The *fylgja* was a person's uniqueness and individuality. The *fylgja* was depicted with a totem spirit. An animal represented a person's *fylgja*, one that was symbolic of their spirit and *hugr*. Since this part of the soul was so distinctive, it died when the person departed this world.

The fourth part of the Scandinavian soul was the *hamingja*. This aspect was inherited natural tendencies that continued from generation to generation. This quality helped shape what a person would be successful at doing and what they would be unsuccessful at or struggle to perform.

After a person died, their soul might be transported to different locations. Perhaps the most well known is Valhalla. Heroic warriors entered Odin's hall. There, the warriors prepared for the ultimate battle at Ragnarök.

Freya's domain, Fólkvangr, also housed warriors. Since Freya was able to choose those who entered, Fólkvangr, or Field of the People, was reputed to have a more notable gathering of Vikings. It is believed that warriors in this realm also spent their time readying themselves for the ultimate clash during Ragnarök.

Scandinavians who were not Vikings during their time in the living realm would have had their *hugr* transported to Helheim or Hel. The majority of the Scandinavian souls lived their eternal days in Helheim. Hel's afterworld is separated from this world with gates and a river. Therefore, after a soul enters Helheim, it cannot return. Only the goddess Hel has the power to free a person from death.

An afterworld specifically for the seafaring Norse was found in the realm of Rán. Rán was married to Aegir, the lord of the sea, and her hall in the afterlife included all of the treasures she took from sailors. She captured mariners in her nets and then drowned them, keeping their souls with her at the bottom of the sea.

Rán pulling a seafarer into her net.
https://commons.wikimedia.org/wiki/File:Ran_by_Johannes_Gehrts.jpg

It was also believed that ghosts or reanimated corpses could emanate from burial mounds. These mound dwellers could then become mystical beings. These spirits were either *haugbui* and guarded their family, or they became a *draugr* and left their graves to create problems for their living family members. Some thought *draugrs* were a result of family members not performing the funeral services correctly.

To appease the gods and goddesses, Scandinavians performed a *blót*. This ceremony was held at least four times a year. Scandinavians sought to be seen in a positive light by the gods, so, at a minimum, *blót* rituals were held seasonally. On or near the winter solstice, the spring equinox, the summer solstice, and the autumn equinox, the Scandinavians gathered for a *blót*. If a village was struggling, preparing for battle, or needing assistance, additional *blóts* were conducted.

Rituals were enacted to garner the support of the gods. Ceremonies were held on the land of the local leader or chieftain. This allowed the ruler to display his wealth and power while villagers paid homage to the gods. *Blóts* could be devoted to any or all of the gods. In addition to paying respect to deities, *blóts* could also be dedicated to ancestors or spirits that had the power to assist and guide the village.

Sacrificial feasts of horses, cattle, or pigs were prepared. Blood or *hlaut* from the slain animals was scattered on those present at the ceremony and statues of deities as a representation of life and its power. The food and drink were ceremonially blessed. Then all gathered to eat together, which symbolically included the gods, spirits, or ancestors, at the same table. Goblets of mead were drunk in remembrance of deceased ancestors.

Another connection the Scandinavians made to the gods was living a life of honor. They believed that living a virtuous life would align them with the gods. It was expected that all members of Scandinavian society would follow this code.

Virtues that guided Vikings included courage. Bravery was rewarded by the gods. Entering battles without fear was expected. Living a daily life facing and addressing hardships was a goal for all.

Secondly, everyone should always tell the truth. Lying was viewed as a cowardly action. Being truthful to others and to oneself was important. Standing up and defending one's principles was part of the code of honor. Fidelity or loyalty to one's fellow citizens, warriors, and craftsmen was the basis for all relationships in the Viking world.

Control over one's actions or discipline was another tenet of the nine Viking virtues. Being able to stay strong in challenging situations required discipline. Living within a community, which enhanced one's well-being, was another belief. Hospitality was necessary to develop and sustain relationships within one's family and between families. Treating others with respect was part of this belief partly because one never knew if a god had taken a human form and arrived in the village as a stranger.

Self-reliance was another important rule. Providing for one's family without assistance from others was considered a necessity to be a protective member of society. Everyone had to live a life that capitalized on their talents. Connected to self-reliance was industry. All tasks should be done to the best of one's ability. Laziness was viewed as shameful.

And the ninth tenet of their belief system was perseverance. When facing difficult and adverse situations, the Viking honor system called for tenacity. Through successfully confronting challenges, one's strength of character is born.

The Scandinavians who lived during the Viking Age blended their belief system with daily living. Following the code of conduct connected each person to their community and deities. Harmonizing one's individual and societal actions and inactions kept one in the good graces of the gods and their neighbors.

Chapter 14: Wars of the Gods

Scandinavians in the Viking Age believed in many godly beings. Elves, dwarves, spirits, gods, and goddesses all guided the Vikings. Supernatural creatures had humanlike qualities to them, which made these beings more relatable for the Norse (in this case, those who followed the Norse religion—those living in Sweden, Denmark, and Norway). Developing and maintaining a positive relationship with all non-mortals was important. No one wanted to endure the wrath of a mystical deity.

Gods and goddesses helped the Norse make sense of the natural world that surrounded them. A deity's actions were used to explain phenomena, such as weather events. Oceans and their tides, the flow of rivers, and how mountains rose were understood through stories of gods and goddesses. Myths made it easier to connect to the gods as though they were neighbors of the Vikings. Since the gods had their own personalities, the Norse could appreciate their own interactions with each other.

Most gods and goddesses in Norse mythology are connected to either the Æsir or Vanir tribe. Both tribes have similar gods and goddesses. Their distinction is more in their approach to life. The Æsir family was considered more physical and protective. Its members monitored and manipulated the sky. The Vanir gods were viewed as more compassionate and nature-oriented. They were caretakers of the sea and earth.

Odin was the lead god of the Æsir. This clan was structured similarly to the Viking world. Gods were assigned the task of ensuring that societal accords were followed. The Æsir were talented warriors and saw the ability to fight as an essential skill. These gods practiced and trained in the art of combat and war, which they used when they traveled the world. The Norse people called upon these gods for assistance with wars, births, marriages, deaths, and the roles of each person in society.

Gods and goddesses of the Vanir clan followed a more casual and free-spirited attitude to living. They were adept in the practice and application of sorcery and magic, so they learned spells and potions. Their ability to speak to the dead and use their mystical skills made others leery of them. They provided the Scandinavians with an understanding and appreciation of the seasons and natural occurrences. Their rules of behavior were much more open and less defined. A more laissez-faire view of the world was provided to the Norse through these deities.

The two clans of deities usually did not interact. They peacefully existed and inhabited two different realms. The gods and goddesses of the Æsir lived in Asgard; Vanaheimr was home to the Vanir. That is until Gullveig, a Vanir goddess, entered the realm of the Æsir. Some myths claim that Gullveig was actually Freya in disguise; many other stories tell of Gullveig as being a separate goddess from Freya.

Either way, the potent magic of Gullveig precipitated the first war of the gods, which was fought between the Æsir and Vanir.

Similar to earthly women who performed the magical art of *seidr*, Gullveig traveled from village to village, enchanting others with her potent witchcraft. Gullveig's spells and potions beguiled the Æsir. Initially, they welcomed Gullveig into Asgard and treated her as a special guest. However, her magic was so strong that some of the Æsir craved her spells. Beliefs of their loyalty and honor were being cast aside since they coveted her magic.

Some in Asgard recognized the alluring and dangerous reach of Gullveig. Fearful of the control she was garnering over their world, the Asgardians assembled the members of the ruling council. They unanimously agreed that Gullveig could not continue spreading her *seidr*, so the council decided to kill her.

Their first attempt to execute Gullveig was to use spears. Unbeknownst to the executioners, the talented sorceress had cast a spell on herself. She was immune to weapons penetrating her body, so she survived.

Next, the Æsir tried to burn Gullveig at the stake. The flames engulfed her, and Gullveig perished in excruciating pain. Again, her formidable talents saved her, as she arose from her cinders. Not ready to concede defeat, the Æsir tried again. Once more, Gullveig resurrected herself from her dying embers.

By this time, her fellow Vanir gods and goddesses had heard of her plight. Infuriated at the actions of the Æsir, the Vanir declared war. The war commenced with Oden throwing his spear into the troops of the Vanir. Vikings mimicked this action in their opening battle scenes. The Viking leader hurled his spear at the opposing forces and announced that Viking causalities were in honor of and sacrifice to Odin.

Intense fighting followed the opening lob. With their background and training, the Æsir were expected to be victorious. The Æsir brutally fought the Vanir. However, the Vanirs' skill in employing magical arts created an evenly contested war. The home realms of both sides suffered extensive damage. Later myths tell stories of rebuilding Asgard's fortifications. Neither side would yield.

Odin throws his spear at the Vanir host.
https://commons.wikimedia.org/wiki/File:%C3%86sir-Vanir_war_by_Fr%C3%B8lich.jpg

Realizing that no one would win, Odin signaled for a truce. Gods representing both sides met to negotiate a peace treaty. Following traditional Viking practices, the two groups agreed to swap hostages or captured gods with each other. This symbolic act was to further solidify the expectations of coexisting in peace.

In the deal, the Æsir leaders sent Hoenir and Mimir to live among the Vanir as honorary members. In exchange, Njord and his children, Freya and her twin brother Freyr, went to live in Asgard with the Æsir.

Njord, Freya, and Freyr were widely accepted among the Æsir. Freya shared her skills of *seith* or magic with her new clan. She taught others in the Æsir magic, including the power to foresee future events. The three assimilated into Asgard and became valued gods and goddesses.

In the Vanir world of Vanaheimr, the trade was not as effective. Hoenir and his counsel, Mimir, were sent to the Vanir to provide experience that the Æsir gods had. When Hoenir was invited to provide guidance, he was either silent or asked others for their input. The Vanir gods were surprised. They had been led to believe that Hoenir would be a great asset.

What the Vanir deities did not realize was that Hoenir was slow-witted. He relied completely on Mimir for guidance. To hide this from the Vanir, Mimir told Hoenir not to answer the Vanirs' questions or provide suggestions. Instead, Mimir advised Hoenir to seek the input of others. By doing this, no one would know that Mimir did all the thinking for the two of them.

After realizing that Hoenir had no thought capacity without Mimir, the Vanir became suspicious. They did not trust Mimir and knew Hoenir was not a wise leader. The Vanir believed the Æsir had cheated them in the peace treaty, so they killed Hoenir and decapitated Mimir. They sent Mimir's head to Odin.

Odin was able to revitalize Mimir's head by applying magical herbs and chanting spells. Mimir continued to advise Odin and keep him apprised of events.

The leaders of the two clans met again to avoid restarting the war. Both sides felt they had been wronged in the peace treaty. However, both the Vanir and Æsir understood that reigniting the conflict would result in more fierce fighting and damage to the kingdoms. So, they agreed to continue the truce.

This ceremonial peace was sealed with the archaic process of producing and drinking mead. All the gods were provided with berries. Each deity was expected to chew the berries they were given. Then each of them took turns spitting the mashed berries into one vessel. Magically, the mixture of the spittle from the gods transformed into Kvasir, which are fermented berries.

Kvasir was extremely intelligent and wise, and he traveled through all nine realms of the universe, sharing his knowledge. He astutely responded to all questions posed to him. Kvasir spent his life roaming the cosmos. He bestowed his insights on everyone he encountered.

Unfortunately, Kvasir was murdered by two dwarves so they could obtain his wisdom. Fjalar and Galar emptied Kvasir's body of all its blood. They then filled three separate containers with the blood. By mixing the blood with honey, Fjalar and Galar concocted a new mead: the Mead of Poetry. Anyone who drank from this special mead would be infused with some of Kvasir's wisdom and could craft poems. This was how poetry came into the world.

The peace between the Vanir and Æsir was not affected by the dwarves' actions.

Another part of the deities' agreement was to share humankind's veneration. The two clans were viewed as equal. Odin became the leader of all the gods. Vanir gods and goddesses continued to reside in Asgard, with the Vanir deities retaining their residences in Vanaheimr.

Gods were not expected to engage in combat again until Ragnarök. At the end of this last battle of the world, the world would end. Many different versions of the myth exist; however, in all iterations, humans and gods suffer dire consequences.

The bravest of the Viking warriors fought with Odin. After their deaths on the battlefield, the Valkyries selected the most talented and fiercest combatants to reside and train in Valhalla. In the spectacular hall at Valhalla, the chosen Vikings would be surrounded by glistening spears and shields made of gold. Every day, the Vikings prepared and practiced for Ragnarök. Each night, the Valkyries provided a feast for the Vikings. Then they healed all the wounds inflicted during their daily training sessions.

Signs of the approaching battle would be sent to the combatants. One indicator was three years without summer and wars in Midgard during the three winters. This would be followed by a brutally harsh winter called Fimbulvetr; snow would fall throughout the entire year. After the Great Winter, the sun would no longer shine and warm the earth. People would become desperate for food and warmth, which would lead to an abandonment of ethics and laws as humankind fought to survive.

The giants would be alerted that Ragnarök had begun when the rooster, Fjalar, crowed its warning. Another rooster would awaken the dead. Gullinkambi, Valhalla's rooster, would notify the gods. Combatants would meet in Vigrid, the realm for battles, where the battle to end all battles would begin.

The wolves, Sköll and Hati, will steal the sun and moon from the skies and ravage them. The erupting violence jolts the stars from the sky. Blackness envelops the world, and all the trees and mountains collapse when Yggdrasil, the huge tree that keeps the cosmos united, shudders.

The Wolves Pursuing Sol and Mani.
https://commons.wikimedia.org/wiki/File:The_Wolves_Pursuing_Sol_and_Mani.jpg

Loki, who had been punished for causing the death of the god Baldr, was chained to rocks on an island. The commencement of Ragnarök will loosen his binds and free him. Then he will board and captain the ship *Naglfar*, which was filled with giants. Loki will sail the ship, which is constructed from the nails of dead men, into battle. Since the earth will be flooded, Loki can navigate his ghost ship wherever he wants.

The wolf, Fenrir, will bust free from the chains that restrained him. He will rummage the earth, causing death and destruction to all in his path. Eventually, Fenrir will encounter Odin. With his valiant warriors from Valhalla at his side, Odin and Fenrir engage in a ferocious battle. However, Fenrir will be victorious. Vidar, one of Odin's sons, will seek revenge. Vidar wears a shoe sewn from all the leather scraps thrown out by shoemakers. The depth of the shoe will enable Vidar to open Fenrir's mouth. With the wolf's jaw spread wide, Vidar thrusts his sword through Fenrir's throat. This will kill the vicious wolf.

Jörmungandr, the serpent that wraps itself around Midgard, will emerge from the chaotic waters of the sea. Once in battle, Jörmungandr seeks Thor, his longtime adversary. With a mighty thrust of his hammer, Thor massacres the massive serpent. Before Jörmungandr dies, he will douse Thor with enough venom to kill him.

Loki will die at the hands of Heimdall. The giant Surt and the god Freyr will both perish in their fight. By the end of the fighting, most of the gods will have died. Much of the world will burn, most humans will perish, and animals will die, but the monsters will depart from the world. The remains of the earth will sink into the rising sea.

Some tales say this is the end, but in most versions, the earth rises from its watery demise. The human race is repopulated by the children of Lif and Lifthrasir. The gods Vali and Vidar and the sons of Thor and Hoenir remain to guide the humans. They move to the realm of Idavoll. Balder and Hoder will be brought back from the dead to join the other gods in Idavoll.

Chapter 15: The Nine Realms in Norse Mythology

Vikings worshiped numerous gods. Polytheistic beliefs permitted and encouraged everyone from thralls to chieftains to revere different deities. The gods and goddesses had humanlike qualities that made them accessible to understand; these deities could even die. All of the gods and goddesses had their own personalities. Imperfections and flaws in their lives and decisions made them real to those who revered them.

The Norse belief system was framed around the World Tree or Yggdrasil. Emanating from Yggdrasil were the homes of all the beings that were part of the Norse world. There are different thoughts today about where each of the realms would have been in relation to the World Tree. However, the most current research agrees that the Scandinavians believed in Yggdrasil, the nine realms, and the beings who inhabited the realms.

The World Tree, Yggdrasil.
https://commons.wikimedia.org/wiki/File:The_Ash_Yggdrasil_by_Friedrich_Wilhelm_Heine.jpg

Standing at the center of the Norse universe was Yggdrasil. The massive tree was surrounded by the nine realms. These nine worlds were interconnected and held together by Yggdrasil. All the parts of Yggdrasil were significant in maintaining this cosmos. The longevity and health of the world were dependent upon the well-being of the tree.

The translation of the tree's name is Odin's horse. *Yggr* equates to the word "terrible," which is a name that was used to refer to the god Odin. *Drasil*, or "horse," is the second part of the tree's name. The tree is named for the occasion when Odin sought to understand runes. To Odin, the runes or letters represented knowledge.

Housed within the upper branches of Yggdrasil was Asgard, the realm of Odin. From his position, he could view the Norns, three women who shaped and manipulated fate. The Norns engraved runes on the trunk of Yggdrasil to control fate. Odin was jealous of their powers and sought a way to gain that knowledge for himself.

The message in the runes could only be divulged to someone who could prove themself worthy of obtaining the wisdom. So, Odin impaled himself with his spear. Odin then hung himself from a branch of Yggdrasil. For nine days and nights, one for each of the nine realms, Odin hung from the World Tree. Then, from the depths of Yggdrasil, the runes revealed their shapes and meanings to Odin. This knowledge made Odin one of the most powerful gods.

In addition to carving the runes on Yggdrasil that impacted all nine realms, the Norns were responsible for ensuring the health of the World Tree. Water from Urd's well was sprinkled on Yggdrasil's roots daily by the Norns to keep the tree healthy. Mud was gathered from the area around the well and used to repair areas of the roots that were damaged by animals and decay. Healthy roots were essential for uniting all parts of the world.

The Norns represented the past, present, and future. They were respectively named Urd, Verdandi, and Skuld. Together, the three determined the fate of one's life. One Norn spun the thread of life, the next one measured its length, and the last Norn decided when the thread should end.

The daily gatherings of the gods were held at the Well of Urd. Gods rode into the meetings on their horses, except for Thor, who arrived in his goat-driven chariot. At these daily discussions, the gods talked about justice with the Norns. The Norns captured the plans in their runic writing.

The second well feeding Yggdrasil was Mimisbrunnr, or Mimir's well, which provided insight and knowledge. Drinking this potent holy water required one to make a sacrifice to the well. Odin exchanged one of his eyes for the opportunity to drink from the well and gain wisdom. He visited the well often to confer with Mimir's head. Mimir, the god of wisdom, provided guidance to Odin during their discussions. The root from this well led to Jotunheim, which was the homeland of the frost giants.

Hvergelmir existed before time and was believed to be the original well in the Norse world. Waters from this well connected to the realm of Niflheim, where the Norse believed that the first signs of life emerged. When the World Tree lived in the great void or Ginnungagap, the icy temperature of the abyss froze the water and created Niflheim. When the realm of fire or Muspelheim arose near Niflheim, a vapor appeared. This fog was the progenitor of all beings.

The first known giant, Ymir, emerged from this mist. He produced additional giants while he slept. Icy surfaces continued to melt from the heat from which Audhumla, a cow, was uncovered. To feed herself, Audhumla licked the ice that surrounded her. The first of the Æsir clan, Buri, was discovered in the melting ice.

Buri, the progenitor of the gods, had a son named Borr. Borr married Bestla, the daughter of Bolthorn, one of the frost giants. Together, Borr and Bestla had three children. All three were part god and part giant. Their children were Odin, Vili, and Vé.

The three brothers were concerned about how rapidly Ymir could create offspring. Ymir's descendants greatly outnumbered the half-god and half-giant beings in the world. Odin and his brothers decided they needed to kill Ymir to better balance the world. The gory battle resulted in Ymir's blood drowning all but two giants: Bergelmir and his wife. They became the ancestors of all giants born after Ymir's death.

Odin and his brothers used the remains of Ymir to erect the world and the other seven realms. The flow of Ymir's blood created the waterways. His skin and muscles were transformed into soil and land. Mountains were formed from his bones. Ymir's teeth were used for rocks. Flora and fauna were shaped from his hair.

Then the brothers took Ymir's head and tossed it. From his brains came the clouds, and the sky was made from Ymir's skull. Embers of fire were snatched from Muspelheim and tossed inside his skull to serve as the stars in the sky.

Though Odin and his brothers acted quickly, Ymir's body was massive. While they worked, worms formed in Ymir's remains. The trio used the worms to form the dwarves. The brothers were concerned about the stability of what they had created, so they picked four dwarves to hold up the sky. The four dwarves were sent in four opposite directions. They were as follows: Nordi (north), Sundri (south), Austri (east), and Vestri (west).

Since their work was completed with Ymir's body, Odin and his brothers began constructing the remaining realms.

Located near Asgard is Alfheim, or the land of the elves. The Vanir god Freyr reigned over this realm. Freyr was the Norse god of the harvest, fertility, and hunting. Elves had the responsibility of assisting Freyr. They had the ability to impact the harvest. Elves could also affect fertility by impeding one's chances of pregnancy or working to assist with fertility.

The elves were incredibly beautiful creatures and illuminated their surroundings. Their presence motivated others to create artistic endeavors, including music and poetry. Alfheim was seen as a realm of brightness, harmony, and calmness.

Dancing Elves, a depiction of Alfheim.
https://commons.wikimedia.org/wiki/File:%C3%84lvalek.jpg

Also known as caretakers, the elves could be called upon for guidance, assistance, and protection. If one found themselves in a crisis, these guardian angels would be there to help.

Odin created a home for himself, Asgard, and presided over it with Frigga. All the gods and goddesses of the Æsir clan live in Asgard. The realm was home to fabulous palaces and halls. Asgard was also home to Valhalla. This elegant hall with 540 doors accepted warriors who died valiantly in battle. Those selected by Odin were transported to Valhalla by the Valkyries. These beautiful female guides carried the warriors to Asgard. Warriors not chosen by Odin would go to Fólkvangr, which was located within the boundaries of Asgard. They were housed in the hall of Sessrumnir and ruled by Freya.

Valaskjalf was another hall in Asgard built for Odin. Its roof was made from pure silver. Within Valaskjalf is Hlidskjalf, Odin's throne. From this vantage point, Odin could see what was happening in the other realms.

A fiery rainbow bridge named Bifrost connected the two domains of Asgard and Midgard. Any of the gods and goddesses could move from their world to that of the humans. Asgard was a realm of law and order. Its entrance was guarded by Heimdall, who protected the world of the gods.

The realm for all the dead warriors who were not worthy of Valhalla or Fólkvangr was Hel of Helheim. Those who did not live an honorable life in Midgard were also sent here. Not to be confused with Christian hell, Hel was headed by and named for Loki's daughter, the queen of death.

Sensing that Loki's children would cause problems for the other gods and goddesses, Odin relocated them from Asgard. Odin moved each of them to areas of the world where their ability to create havoc would be minimized. Hel, which means "hidden" in Old Norse, was selected to live in Helheim. Hel's brother, the serpent Jörmungandr, was hurled into the ocean surrounding Midgard; her other bother, Fenrir the wolf, was shackled until Ragnarök.

Access to Helheim was restricted to one lengthy treacherous pathway. Traversing this desolate path included crossing a river of clashing weapons. Once one found the bridge to cross over, then, out of the ominous mist, appeared the one entranceway in the wall that enveloped the realm of Hel.

The home or realm of the giants (the Jötnar) was Jotunheim. Jotunheim is depicted as a chaotic and lawless world. It was located beyond the realm of order. Sometimes, Jotunheim is also known as Utgard; other sources portray Utgard as an area within the realm of the giants. Since Jotunheim housed the giants, the span of the land was massive, expanding from Asgard to Midgard. The River Ifing separated the orderly world of Asgard from the disorderly realm of the giants. Though Jotunheim is portrayed as a world that has a perpetual winter, the magical waterway never froze.

Since the beginning of creation, when Odin and his brothers killed Ymir, the giants sought revenge. As adversaries of the Æsir, the giants continually warred with Odin and the other gods. Frequently, the Jötnar tried invading Asgard, desiring to kill the gods who resided there. Once that task was completed, the Jötnar would kidnap the goddesses and take them back to Jotunheim to wed. Most gods and goddesses did not willingly travel to Jotunheim.

Situated between Jotunheim and Asgard was the world created for humans. Midgard, or Middle Earth, was separated from Jotunheim by Jörmungandr. The serpent was another of Loki's children that Odin could not trust; Odin cast Jörmungandr into the oceans to live until the final battle of the gods.

From Ymir's hair, Odin created flora and vegetation on Midgard. Then Odin and his two brothers, Vili and Vé, formed the first humans. The trio of brothers shaped the tree into the first humans. Ask, Midgard's first man, was shaped from an ash tree. An elm tree provided the basis for Embla, the first female. All other humans were descendants of Ask and Embla.

The realm of fire, from which the sparks emanated to cause the creation of Ymir, is known as Muspelheim. Surtr, a fire giant, ruled this hostile world. A mortal enemy of the Æsir gods, Surtr waits for the day when he can set the other realms ablaze with his fire. At the end of the world, Surtr will play a key role in the destruction of the realms. He and his sons will set Asgard ablaze; he will also set fire to Yggdrasil, seeking to destroy all life within the World Tree.

Also part of the creation myth was the world opposite to Muspelheim. In Niflheim, or the mist world, a realm of cold, snow, and ice can be found. These two realms gave birth to Ymir from the abyss of Ginnungagap, which began all creation. A spring located in Niflheim, Hvergelmir, fed Yggdrasil and sustained all life. The dragon, Nidhogg, protected the spring of life. He acted as a sentry and kept the dead and living separate from each other.

Dwarves who arose from the bugs from Ymir's rotting corpse were provided a home in Svartalfheim. Since they emanated from insects within the giant's dead body, their world was fashioned so that the dwarves could reside in dark caves and underground. Though they were small in stature and lived in a world without much light, they produced much beauty and magic.

Dwarves were master craftsmen who were adept at a multitude of trades. They were able to make jewelry, work as blacksmiths, and shape all types of metal. The dwarves gave the gods many magical and powerful gifts. They are credited with having created Draupnir, Odin's enchanted ring, and his spear, Gungnir. For Thor, the dwarves fashioned Mjolnir, his hammer. A ship that could be folded into a pocket, *Skidbladnir*, was created for Freyr.

The last of the realms was Vanaheimr, the home of the Vanir. These tranquil gods immersed themselves in the world of untamed nature. Vanaheimr was where the Vanir continued to reside after their war with the Æsir. The Vanir were known for their ability to see into the future. They were called upon by mortals living in Midgard to assist with good harvests, as the Vanir were able to affect the sun, rain, and wind.

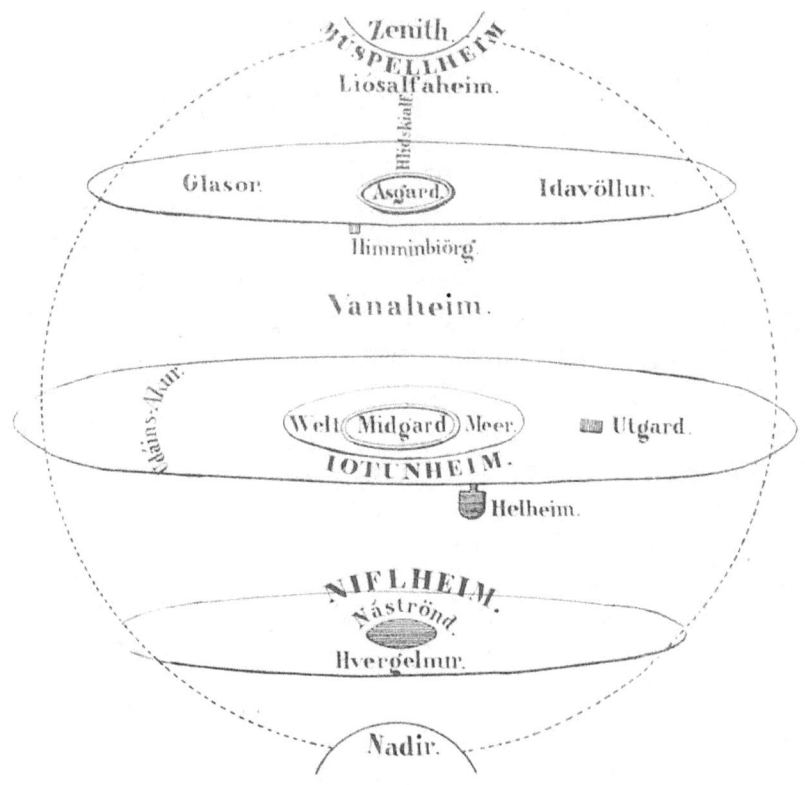

Cosmos of Norse mythology.
https://commons.wikimedia.org/wiki/File:WHEATON(1844)_The_Cosmos_in_the_Norse_mythology.jpg

The nine realms will coexist until the day of judgment when Ragnarök commences.

Chapter 16: Symbols and Possessions of the Norse Gods and Goddesses

Connecting all nine realms of the Norse world was Yggdrasil, also known as the World Tree. This one tree bound together life and death, good and evil, and heaven and earth. Therefore, Yggdrasil was one of the key symbols of the Norse people.

Vikings believed that Yggdrasil and other symbols were a way of asking the gods for assistance. Each symbol had its own meaning and purpose. Depending upon the situation in which Vikings found themselves or knew they were embarking upon, they carried their symbol for support and protection.

One symbol the Vikings warriors believed would assist them on their raiding and pillaging voyages was the *vegvisir*. The word for the symbol has roots in *vegur*, for "road" or "path," and *visir*, which means "guide." The *vegvisir* was also referred to as the Viking compass. It has a circular center from which emanates eight rune staves. Many believe these represent compass directions: four staves for the four cardinal points on the compass. The other four symbols correspond to the intercardinal directions.

Vikings began to develop navigational technology. However, for additional support during their long and dangerous voyages, the

Viking compass was drawn on ships before they sailed. The *vegvisir* symbol was supposed to ensure safe passage for the ship and its passengers. Not only did the Viking compass assist ships, but it was also worn as an amulet by those who were seeking guidance in life.

Another ancient Norse symbol that provided protection for the wearer was the Helm of Awe or *Aegishjalmr*. Originating in the Old Norse language, the word *aegis* meant shield, and *hjalmr* meant helm. Similar in design to the *vegvisir*, the *Aegishjalmr* has eight tridents that radiate from a central point. The defensive posture of the spike-tipped spears gives the appearance of a shield guarding the center. Sometimes, the *Aegishjalmr* was depicted with serpents in the outer circle that would incapacitate their enemies before attacking them.

The symbol itself was thought to inflict terror in those who saw it. Vikings etched the Helm of Awe on their weapons, armor, and helmets. Some warriors drew *Aegishjalmr* on their foreheads with blood as they prepared for battle.

Scandinavian tales say that the Helmet of Awe was originally owned by Hreidmar, the giant. Hreidmar possessed much gold, which he had received from Odin. The giant had demanded the gold as payment for Odin's murder of Hreidmar's son. When Odin gave the giant the gold, he placed a curse on it. One of Hreidmar's other sons, Fafnir, killed his father for the gold. Fafnir took the gold and the helmet. With the power of the helmet, Fafnir transformed himself into a dragon so he could guard his golden treasures.

Helm of Awe.
https://commons.wikimedia.org/wiki/File:Aegishjalmr.svg

The valknut is the Slain Warrior's Knot and is often referred to as Odin's symbol. Going into battle with the power of Odin was provided to the Viking warriors by applying the valknut symbol on their bodies, wearing jewelry with it, or inscribing it on their weaponry. Valknut was a powerful symbol that offered protection in battle. If a warrior died while fighting, they were still safeguarded with the valknut symbol. Warriors believed that Odin would be there in their death to receive and greet them at the gates of Valhalla.

Since Odin was a spiritual guide, this symbol was also viewed as a passage from one realm to another or from life to death. Depicted as intertwined triangles, the valknut was also connected to the nine realms of Norse mythology. The three triangles create nine corners or nine lands on the World Tree. Each of the triangles represents different spheres in the cosmos of heaven, hell, and earth. The points of the triangles point upward to Odin's realm of Asgard.

Similar to valknut in its broad, powerful scope was Mjolnir or Thor's hammer. This hammer had the capability to kill and deliver blessings. Thor was indomitable with Mjolnir. Amulets of Mjolnir were worn by Viking warriors to summon the brawn and valor of Thor in battle. These amulets are the most often discovered artifacts at Norse excavation sites. Thor used the power of Mjolnir to safeguard the realm of Asgard from the chaos of other worlds. In his role as protector of the land of the gods, Thor and Mjolnir kept turmoil and confusion at bay with their decisive victories over the giants, trolls, and other menacing beings.

Not only did Mjolnir keep the home of the gods safe and protect warriors, but Thor's hammer was also used by the god to provide blessings. Mjolnir had the power to impede the forces of evil. With this protection from Thor, couples sanctified in marriage were given the gift of fertility. Thor's expansive reach extended to fecundity in the field, granting the people an abundant harvest.

Mjolnir was a result of the trickster god Loki's mischievousness. Always causing trouble, Loki decided to annoy Thor, so he cut Sif's hair as she slept. Sif, Thor's wife, had gorgeous golden tresses. Thor was infuriated by Loki's actions. To defend his wife, Thor threatened to kill Loki. Ever the trickster, Loki promised Thor that he would replace Sif's magnificent locks of hair with ones even more incredible. Thor accepted Loki's deal.

Loki traveled to the realm of the dwarves, Svartalfheim. The dwarves were known for their talent as craftsmen. They agreed to weave strands of gold together to replace Sif's hair. She would once again rule as the goddess of grain and fertility.

While Loki was with the dwarves, he taunted them. Loki told them that they could not make more fabulous pieces than they already had; their abilities had peaked. Accepting the challenge, the dwarves forged Mjolnir. However, Loki did not want them to win the challenge, so he shapeshifted into a fly. He buzzed around and irritated the dwarves as they worked. This caused Thor's hammer to have an unusually short handle.

Though the hammer was flawed, Thor was amazed at its abilities. Loki had fulfilled his part of the bargain and was permitted to live. To hold the handle, Thor had to wear his magical iron gloves. Mjolnir returned to Thor every time he threw it. With his hammer, Thor was almost invincible.

Picture of Thor's hammer found in Sweden.
Ola Myrin, Statens historiska museum/SHM, CC BY 4.0 <https://creativecommons.org/licenses/by/4.0>, via Wikimedia Commons; https://commons.wikimedia.org/wiki/File:Claes_Kurck_Sk%C3%A5ne_hammer_-_HST_DIG55488_original.jpg

The prolific dwarves created other treasures for the gods while Loki was in their realm. As part of his challenge to them, the Sons of Ivaldi, who sewed Sif's golden locks, also crafted two other wonders for the gods. One was *Skidbladnir*, and the other treasure was Gungnir.

The ship, *Skidbladnir*, had magical powers. Some tell of Loki bestowing the ship to the god Freyr; other stories say that Freyr's twin sister, the goddess Freya, was given the ship. Regardless of the owner of *Skidbladnir*, the Sons of Ivaldi, constructed a vessel that could be folded up so small that it could fit in a deity's pocket.

When the ship was unfolded, all the gods had to do was breathe on the miniature ship, and it would expand into a mighty craft. It grew so large that all the gods and goddesses who lived in Asgard could fit on it. Their weaponry, battle gear, and horses were easily stowed on board.

This ship of the Norse gods would magically transport its passengers anywhere. *Skidbladnir* could travel on land and sea in all weather conditions. Whenever its sails were hoisted, *Skidbladnir* was assured of winds that would propel it quickly and effortlessly to its destination. Once at its endpoint, the ship was refolded and inserted into a small pouch.

The dwarves also produced the lethal spear Gungnir. Gungnir was gifted to Odin by Loki after Loki returned from Svartalfheim. Similar to Thor's hammer, when Gungnir was thrown, it would return back to Odin. Also, Gungnir always reached its target and could pierce any material.

Odin used this spear to stab himself when he hung from Yggdrasil to gain knowledge of the runes. This special spear was also the one Odin flung to initiate the Æsir and Vanir war, which makes it a symbol of victory. Viking warriors replicated this action to start all their battles. They threw the first sword and invoked the power of Odin to be with them in battle and at the entrance to Valhalla.

Loki was not satisfied with the treasures he watched the dwarves create. Continuing his trickery, Loki conned two other dwarves into making him more valuables. He told Brokker and Sindri (also known as Eitri) that there was a contest in Asgard to see who was more talented: the Sons of Ivaldi or the two of them. However, these two brothers took a bit more convincing, so Loki bet his head that

Brokker and Sindri were not as gifted as the Sons of Ivaldi.

Seizing the challenge, Brokker and Sindri created three masterpieces, one of which was Mjolnir. Loki transformed into a fly and pestered and distracted the brothers. However, they endured and finished all three items.

From a pigskin, Brokker and Sindri fashioned Gullinbursti, which means "golden bristles." This golden boar was quicker than all other animals except Odin's horse, Sleipnir. Not only was Gullinbursti the second-fastest of all, but it could also speed through all elements, including air and water.

Its hairs were fabricated from gold, so Gullinbursti glowed with shimmers of light in the darkness. A guiding light shined from Gullinbursti to guide Freyr in any lands shrouded in darkness. This gleaming brightness was symbolic of illuminating a pathway in battle for warriors. Many Vikings drew the image of Gullinbursti on their weaponry before battles. Boars were thought to be attendant spirits who escorted the gods to provide protection and good fortune.

Drawing of Gullinbursti and Freyr.
https://commons.wikimedia.org/wiki/File:Freyr_by_Johannes_Gehrts.jpg

Next, the brothers crafted an incredible ring called Draupnir. Every ninth night, Draupnir "dripped" eight brilliant gold rings. Every one of the newly created rings that fell from the one forged by the dwarves was the same size and amount of gold. While the latest rings could not replicate themselves, they gave their owner vast quantities of gold.

Odin, the god of abundance, now possessed a way to gain more wealth. Additional affluence equated to more power. Rings also represented a sign of fidelity, which Odin expected from others who lived in Asgard with him.

When Odin's son Baldr died as a result of Loki's actions, Odin placed Draupnir on Baldr's funeral ship. This is viewed as a sign that Odin realized that Ragnarök would soon commence. Laying the ring on the pyre was Odin's signal of the transition to the new leaders that would emerge.

Another symbol connected to Odin and Viking leaders that bridges the Norse world and the afterlife was a raven. Ravens were visual depictions of the transformation that occurred with death and appeared after battles to feast on the deceased combatants.

Other leaders in the Norse world put symbols of ravens on banners and weaponry. Ravens were perceived as shrewd birds. Their ability to observe all that was around them made them valuable to the Vikings. Kings, warriors, and sailors believed that ravens could see everything.

As Vikings traveled the world, they sailed with ravens. The ravens were caged on the ships. When Vikings needed to know if they were near land, the ravens were released from their cages. If land was nearby, the ravens flew in that direction. If there was not any land in their vicinity, the ravens flew back to the ship.

Odin's twin ravens were Huginn and Muninn. During the day, they flew to each of the realms. With their keen insight and ability to understand the human language, Huginn and Muninn reported all their findings to Odin at the end of each day. They also served as couriers, transmitting messages from other gods and goddesses, supernatural beings, dwarves, or giants to Odin.

Tapestry of Odin with Huginn and Muninn.
https://en.wikipedia.org/wiki/File:Odin_hrafnar.jpg

Huginn, which means thoughts, and Muninn, which means memory, represent Odin's desire for knowledge and learning. For the Vikings, the ravens provided a connection to their ancestors. Keeping deceased family members in one's thoughts and memory provided guidance for humans.

These symbols and more helped the Scandinavians understand their world. Creating visual representations of the gods, goddesses, and their worlds provided a sense of purpose and control. While these gods and goddesses are referred to as characters in Norse mythology, to the people of the Viking Age, these figures were real parts of their religion. Beliefs sustained the Scandinavians in battles, daily life, and death. These images supplied hope for the future and causes to celebrate happiness in life.

Conclusion

The Vikings and Scandinavians left a treasure trove for us. Though the situation in which the Scandinavians found themselves is very different from ours, there are similarities in the human experience. Each person in the Viking Age had hopes and dreams. Each person in today's world has hopes and dreams. Obstacles have hindered people of all ages. The lesson we can learn is how people persevered and adapted.

There are many myths about the Vikings that are not supported by research. One is the horned helmet. Viking warriors were much too practical to waste raw materials to add a feature that did not protect them or injure the enemy. The horned helmet is actually from a costume designer named Carl Doepler. He infused Germanic elements in his creations for Wagner's *The Ring of the Nibelung*.

The Norse gods are prominent in our days of the week. Tuesday is named for Tyr, the Norse god of war; Odin or Woden, the king of the gods, gives us Wednesday; and Thursday is for Thor, the god of the sky and thunder. We find ourselves connected to the Vikings on a daily basis. And by reading more about their exploits and myths, we can find new ways to connect with them.

Here's another book by Enthralling History that you might like

Free limited time bonus

Stop for a moment. We have a free bonus set up for you. The problem is this: we forget 90% of everything that we read after 7 days. Crazy fact, right? Here's the solution: we've created a printable, 1-page pdf summary for this book that you're reading now. All you have to do to get your free pdf summary is to go to the following website:

https://livetolearn.lpages.co/enthrallinghistory/

Once you do, it will be intuitive. Enjoy, and thank you!

Bibliography

Bibliography for Part One accessed beginning August 19, 2022

https://www.english-heritage.org.uk/visit/places/lindisfarne-priory/History/viking-raid/

https://www.englishmonarchs.co.uk/vikings_8.html.

https://www.followthevikings.com/discover/origins.

https://www.historic-uk.com/HistoryUK/HistoryofBritain/Invaders/

http://www.historyofyork.org.uk/themes/viking-invasion

https://www.jorvikvikingcentre.co.uk/the-vikings/

https://www.lifeinnorway.net/scandinavia-before-the-vikings/

https://www.medievalists.net/2021/11/where-did-the-vikings-go-the-decline-of-norse-piracy/

https://www.norden.org/en/information/history-nordic-region "The history of the Nordic Region"

https://nordicperspective.com/history/vikings/viking-origin-story

http://www.scandinavianarchaeology.com/the-vendel-period-the-golden-age-of-the-norse/

https://scandinaviafacts.com/scandinavia-before-the-vikings/

https://weaponsandwarfare.com/2020/07/06/the-great-raid-of-hastein-and-bjorn-ironsides/

https://www.worldhistory.org/article/1321/william-the-conqueror--the-ely-rebellion/

https://www.worldhistory.org/Vikings/

Lassieur, Allison. *The Vikings*. San Diego: Lucent Books 2001.

Bibliography for Part 2 accessed August to October

https://www.britannica.com/topic/Viking-people

https://en.natmus.dk/historical-knowledge/denmark/prehistoric-period-until-1050-ad/the-viking-age/power-and-aristocracy/

https://www.followthevikings.com/discover/culture/viking-literature-and-the-oral-tradition

https://www.historyonthenet.com/viking-society-nobles-medieval-freemen-slaves

https://www.hurstwic.org/history/articles/society/text/social_classes.htm

Lassieur, Allison. The Vikings. San Diego: Lucent Books 2001.

https://www.legendsandchronicles.com/ancient-civilizations/the-vikings/viking-food-and-diet/

https://skjalden.com/viking-social-classes/

https://smarthistory.org/viking-art/

https://sonsofvikings.com/blogs/history/viking-lore-a-quick-intro-to-norse-eddas-and-sagas

https://www.thingsites.com/what-is-a-thing

http://viking.archeurope.com/runes/the-rok-runestone/

https://www.worldhistory.org/Viking_Art/

Bibliography for Part 3 accessed October 2022 to December 2022

Berger, Melvin and Gilda Berger. *The Real Vikings.* National Geographic 2003 Belgium

https://www.berganza.com/periods_viking.html

https://www.britainexpress.com/History/battles/index.htm

https://en.natmus.dk/historical-knowledge/denmark/prehistoric-period-until-1050-ad/the-viking-age/weapons

https://www.historyonthenet.com/viking-weapons-and-armor

https://www.medievalchronicles.com/medieval-history/medieval-history-periods/vikings/famous-viking-battles/

https://regia.org/research/ships/Ships0.htm

https://www.science20.com/the_conversation/vikings_were_craftsmen_too-153378

https://theconversation.com/vikings-were-pioneers-of-craft-and-international-trade-not-just-pillaging-37599

https://vikingsna.org/viking-crafts/

https://viking-styles.com/blogs/history/viking-battles

https://workingtheflame.com/viking-battles/

Bibliography Part 4 accessed December 2022 to January 2023

https://www.celebratepaganholidays.com/general/11-core-nordic-religion-principal-beliefs

Clare, John D. *I Was There – Vikings*. The Bodley Head Children's Books London 1994.

https://englishhistory.net/vikings/viking-burials/

https://www.hurstwic.org/history/articles/mythology/religion/text/practices.htm

https://lufolk.com/blogs/vikings-and-norse-mythology/skidbladnir-best-ship-in-norse-mythology

https://www.newworldencyclopedia.org/entry/Asgard

https://norse-mythology.org/

https://www.su.se/english/news/new-interpretation-of-norse-religion-1.543297

https://thevikingherald.com/article/the-most-important-viking-symbols-a-primer/318

https://vikingr.org/norse-cosmology/yggdrasil

Yasuda, Anita. Explore Norse Myths. White River Junction, VT. Nomad Press, 2015.

https://www.worldhistory.org/article/1836/ten-norse-mythology-facts-you-need-to-know/

www.ingramcontent.com/pod-product-compliance
Lightning Source LLC
Chambersburg PA
CBHW070332010526
44107CB00004B/496